The Pool Bible

The Pool Bible

Nick Metcalfe

CHARTWELL
BOOKS, INC.

This edition published in 2010 by
Chartwell Books, Inc.
A division of Book Sales, Inc.
276 Fifth Avenue Suite 206
New York, NY 10001
USA

ISBN-10: 0-7858-2602-5
ISBN-13: 978-0-7858-2602-6

QTT.POOB

A Quintet book
Copyright © Quintet Publishing Limited
All rights reserved.

This book was conceived, designed, and produced by
Quintet Publishing Limited
The Old Brewery
6 Blundell Street
London N7 9BH
United Kingdom

Project Editors: Robert Davies, Asha Savjani
Designer: Allen Boe
Illustrator: Stuart Holmes
Art Director: Michael Charles
Managing Editor: Donna Gregory
Publisher: James Tavendale

Printed in China by Midas Printing International Limited

Contents

Foreword

By Gareth Potts

Three Times World Eight-Ball Champion

I've always loved playing pool, and started at a younger age than most, when I was just seven. I grew up in a pub, where the game was always being played, and at first I had to stand on a beer crate in order to play.

When I was bought a pool table for my bedroom I could happily spend many hours learning about the game and trying to improve my skills. I was fascinated by pool and always wanted to play more. It wasn't long before it became clear I had real talent for the game, and soon I was playing, and winning, junior tournaments. I won four big tournaments in 2000, including the Junior World Championships. I became the youngest person ever to qualify for the England team, as I began to make my mark in the professional game.

I have won many big tournaments over the years, including the World Eight-Ball Championships three times, and have reached the top of the world rankings. I am still the only man to have won the world title three times, and the only man to retain it.

Despite these successes, I have never lost my essential love for the sport, with all its intricacies and peculiarities. The great thing about pool is that you can walk into most pubs or bars and find a table.

Most people have had a go at playing at least once in their lives, and it remains a great social game.

It is still one of the most popular sports across the world.

The joy of pool is first and foremost to simply play the game, but I don't think you need to reach my level to want to win.

Whenever you see the game being played, whether at the World Championships or in your local bar, the competition is fierce.

We are all aware of the frustrations sometimes associated with this sport. I have taken part in exhibitions recently, and nearly every bar or club I play in operates under slightly different rules. Then there's the agonizing sight of watching your opponent clear the balls, sometimes benefitting from a piece of luck that you can't do anything about.

This book will give you the perfect introduction to the game, outlining the basics of pool and all the equipment you will need to start playing. When you find that your game is improving, you will want to learn some of the more advanced shots and tactics needed to succeed.

The Pool Bible also explains the various forms of the game, and you will soon see

that eight-ball and nine-ball pool are very different.

There is a fascinating guide to the history of pool, and some of the great players that have played it over the past century.

Anything that can promote pool is something that all the top players welcome, as we believe that the sport can become even stronger and enjoy a wider profile in the years to come.

If you're a beginner to this game, or have been playing for a number of years, I'm sure you will find this book extremely useful, and a very enjoyable read.

Gareth Potts after winning the World Eight-Ball Championships in 2007.

Chapter One:
THE HISTORY OF POOL

Most people have tried it once, and millions enjoy it regularly. Pool has undoubtedly been one of sport's great success stories. How did this most popular of all table games originate?

The game of pool has been around for many years, originally evolving from billiards, which was played as long ago as the 16th Century. Above, a line of boys take their aim at the Boys' Billiards Championship in England, December 1937.

The World of Pool

Of all the many hundreds of sports that are played throughout the world, pool remains one of the most accessible and universal. Played in all corners of the globe, and by people of all ages and backgrounds, it is a game that can genuinely call itself classless.

Walk into a bar in Buenos Aires or Bognor, Buffalo or Beijing, and you will see people playing this most enjoyable of games, happily whiling away a whole evening around the table.

Whether you are playing in competition or just for fun, the common theme is sheer

Young men play pool at a riverside billiards hall in Jinghong, China

enjoyment. There are of course so many aspects of the game to intrigue and fascinate, not least the constant surprise at the differences in rules (see page 208 for general rules); not only from country to country, town to town, but sometimes from bar to bar.

The simplicity of pool is in many ways its magic. The size of the table and pockets give even the relative novice a chance of success, and a person new to the game is not usually put off from returning to play again.

Other cue-based games do not always lend themselves so easily to different skill levels. Many people remember how daunting it was when they first played on a full-size snooker table—for some people that feeling never really goes away. Aficionados of billiards will always staunchly defend their game, but the fact remains that for many millions of people, nothing compares to the excitement of playing pool.

And millions regularly try their luck at the game, in dozens of countries. Pool halls and clubs are a particular feature of life in America, both in the big cities and small towns—in fact their presence is now almost part of folklore and a symbol of the country's soul. Across Europe, the game is also huge. Pubs of all shapes and sizes in Britain have a pool table on the premises, and thousands of people will often visit an establishment solely on the basis that they can enjoy the game there.

As the game has grown more popular, pool halls have sprouted up all over the world. There can be no doubt that it is now the most popular international table game played. Pool has developed something of a glamorous image—the feeling that it is a cool pastime—largely thanks to films like *The Hustler*, the brilliant 1961 movie starring Paul Newman as "Fast Eddie" Felson (see image below). At one time, most people used to joke that being good at the game was the result of a "misspent youth," but they seem to say it less nowadays.

And as time has gone on, as is the case with most sports, skills have developed and improved. Players at the top of the sport amaze crowds with the quality of their play, and even at the more fun levels people are not just more skillful than they used to be, but more thoughtful about the game; more aware of the tactical play needed to succeed.

Even in an ever-changing world, when all traditional pursuits and interests (and pool must be bracketed in that category) need to fight to maintain their place, the game shows no sign of losing any of its popularity. Indeed, the

Actor Paul Newman on the set of *"The Hustler,"* 1961.

The game of pool is expanding fast, particularly in the Far East. Every year, thousands of people in the world's new superpower, China, are being introduced to the delights of the game.

opposite is true. But before thinking about the future, it is sometimes necessary to look back, and the history of pool is rich and varied.

THE ORIGINS OF POOL

If someone were to hazard a guess as to the length of time pool had been in existence in one form or another, they might well have suggested 150 or 200 years—but they would have been miles out with that guess. It has to be said that the exact origins of the game remain a matter of open speculation, claim, and counter-claim. What we can state with certainty is that the game developed from the game of billiards, which

was played on tables as long ago as the 16th century.

There is some evidence that, many hundreds of years before that, balls were in existence that were used for a similar purpose, particularly in France, but the games played are thought to be closer to today's bowls and croquet than pool.

Some people like to think of pool originating in the deep south of America, with freed slaves emulating their old masters in playing the games. Others see its origins in the speak-easy days of prohibition. The truth would seem to be more interesting than the myths.

Billiards

Pool very clearly has its roots in billiards, a favorite game of the Spanish explorer Captain Ferdinand de Soto, who landed on the Florida coast in 1539 and introduced the game a year later. More proof of the antiquity of billiards comes from Virginia, where as far back as 1607, the English Cavaliers, escaping from the wrath of Oliver Cromwell, found settling down at night easier after a frame or two, as did the French Huguenots who settled in South Carolina in 1690.

The game persevered in its original form even after the War of Independence, when it was still being played on tables imported by British army officers. While it was mentioned earlier that one of the attractions of pool is its classless nature, it couldn't be seriously argued that the game came from humble origins, with almost all of the people that played the game in the 16th century being wealthy aristocrats.

Three hundred years ago, the tables were primitive by today's standards. The bed was made from oak and covered in a coarse baize. The rails fared no better and were made from a woolen list. The balls were generally turned from ivory and rarely matched in size or weight. In time, however, the equipment gradually improved.

1675
The game of billiards has already been growing in popularity, especially in England, and in this year the game's first known rulebook is published.

Edwin Kentfield, an Englishman from Brighton, and the American industrialist John Thurston designed a slate bed table with rails (albeit rudimentary) made from flannel stuffed with cotton waste. This new table was first used in the early 19th century and upgraded by replacing the rails with the new rubber type in 1845.

Shakespeare mentions billiards in the opening scenes of *Antony and Cleopatra*, when Charmian is asked by Cleopatra if she would like a game. Below: "Playing Billiards," an oil painting by Louis Leopold Boilly, 1807.

Developments in the Game

John Thurston was also responsible for the development and introduction of the first composition balls. The cost of the ivory type was making the game almost exclusively a sport for the very well-off. By 1894, the new Bonzoline composition balls were in play.

This move didn't arrive a moment too soon, since by then some 20,000 elephants were being slaughtered annually to feed the demand for ivory billiard balls. Can you imagine the outcry there would be if this was still happening today?

The cue changed as well. Originally called a mace, the craftsmanship of the wood turners converted it to a cue. A key feature in the development of the humble cue was the addition of a leather tip, invented by the French player Francois Mingaud.

John Carr, an Englishman from Bath, realized the potential of the new tip by chalking it, and was soon impressing spectators with his incredible display of cue ball control. It was the first time that people had seen the draw shot. Carr was happy to provide players, at not inconsiderable cost, with his magical "twisting chalk."

1807
Francois Mingaud studied the game in a Paris prison, and is able to show off his new tip for the first time when released in this year.

EARLY GAMES

The game of pyramids involved a triangle of 15 red balls. The winner was the first player to pot eight balls (this game would work pretty well today, and would certainly put an end to some of the squabbles over rules).

Life pool was the first to use different colored balls other than the white, red, and black balls. It was a game played by more than two players. The object of the game was basically to be the last man standing. Each player would be designated a colored ball at the start of the game, and would lose a "life" when another player potted that color. If you lost three lives you would be eliminated from the game, until there was only one player remaining.

The game of black pool differed slightly from the early game of pyramids, with, as the name suggests, the addition of a black ball. This would be placed halfway up the table. As is the case in some forms of the game today, potting it was extremely valuable.

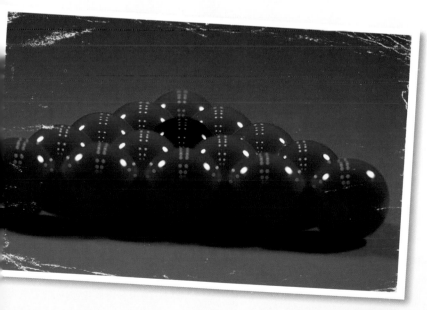

Snooker

Snooker, which was played with 15 red balls and six other colored balls (as it still is today), was developed from the various table games. A young man serving in India in the 19th century, who would later have a rather important namesake, is credited with inventing the game. *The Oxford Dictionary of National Biography* records the important part Neville Chamberlain played in the history of cue sports:

While serving at Jubbulpore in 1875 Chamberlain developed a new variation of black pool by introducing colored balls into the game. It was dubbed snooker —a derogatory nickname given to first-year cadets studying at the Royal Military Academy at Woolwich that Chamberlain had heard about from a young Royal Artillery subaltern visiting the mess.

Chamberlain later retorted to a fellow player who had failed to pot a colored ball: "Why, you're a regular snooker." While explaining the term to his fellow officers Chamberlain, to mollify the officer concerned, remarked that they were all "snookers at the game" and the name snooker or snooker's pool immediately stuck.

As the various innovations took shape, it wasn't long before the game spread to America and Europe. Snooker struggled to establish itself in Britain in the early days, and for many years had to play second fiddle to the more popular

1885
British billiards champion John Roberts is said to have traveled to India to meet Chamberlain, and then introduced the game of snooker on his return.

game of billiards. But when it did become more established, snooker went on to become one of the most popular sports in Britain over the last century—during its golden years of the 1970s and 1980s millions of television viewers were hooked.

Snooker's history can be traced back to the days of British rule in India. The game was first played in Jabalpur in 1875, a hybrid game based on billiards and the Indian games of black pool and life pool.

And today, as with pool, snooker's fastest growing market is in the Far East, where China's best players are among the most well-known people in the whole country, and are often hero-worshipped by young and old alike.

The game of pool in America also has its origins in snooker. This is not without its irony, since snooker has never properly taken off in the United States. The game spread rapidly to its many billiard halls. In practical terms, the tables were often simply too big to be properly accommodated in many of the halls, and were cut down in size.

The new composition balls were far less expensive and more readily available than the older ivory sort, and snooker soon replaced billiards on the small tables. Due to the fact that tables were now smaller, the six colored balls were soon left out of play, leaving 15 balls in a pyramid. The game of pool was being developed.

1927

Snooker's first World Championship is held, with the final in the English city of Birmingham. The legendary Joe Davis, who helped to organize the event, emerges as the winner.

1985

An amazing British television audience of 18.5 million watches after midnight as Dennis Taylor beats Steve Davis to win the world snooker title. This is still widely regarded as the sport's finest hour.

Snooker

19

Early Forms of Pool

Among the earlier forms of the game was straight rail. This was essentially the game of carom billiards, played with three balls and no pockets. In simple terms, the key to the game was caroming, or cannoning, one's own cue ball into your opponent's cue ball and the object ball.

There was also the game of 15-ball pool. In this game each ball had a numerical value, with the total of all the balls in the pack 120 and the winner being the first to reach 61. The game of continuous pool developed from this, where one point was scored per ball and matches typically played over several racks.

STRAIGHT POOL

When this evolved into straight pool, the sport was beginning to establish itself. The most popular form of straight pool became 14.1, which is still widely viewed as the classic form of the game, and was played by many of the early greats. Several people do still play this form of the game today.

In simple terms the game is played until there is one cue ball and one object ball remaining on the table. The 14 potted balls will be re-racked and in the new game a player will try to pot the 15th ball and carom into the new rack.

1765
The first billiard room is built in England. A game of one-pocket, with one hole and four balls, is played. In America players enjoyed a more developed version of one-pocket and four-ball billiards, played with four balls and four pockets.

The reason for the high number of games often needed to win is that a player usually requires a points total far in excess of the 15 points available on the table. The name 14.1 can be explained by the way that games can conclude and start again.

1910

Jerome Keogh, a great champion of continuous pool, is widely credited with inventing straight pool, by simply suggesting that the last ball of each rack be used as a "break ball" for the next rack.

1888

Continuous pool replaces 15-ball pool as the championship game, with the game's organizers believing it was fairer to count the number of balls pocketed by a player and not their numerical value.

You may have needed to "nominate a pocket" when attempting to pot the final ball, especially if you have played pool for some years. In straight pool, the pocket has to be called every time, which is why (unlike in today's more usual forms of the game) the general idea of a break shot was to play safe.

The Game Evolves

As pool developed and grew in the last century, it wasn't surprising that faster forms of the game evolved, for practical reasons, as much as anything else. Eight-ball and nine-ball pool remain the most widely played of these today. Nine-ball is the game which is much more commonly played in America than Europe, particularly in the professional game. It is played on slightly bigger tables than eight-ball.

Most of the better-known global pool tournaments, certainly those that are televised, use the nine-ball form of the game. That is not to say that the nine-ball game isn't popular in certain parts of Europe, notably Scandinavia and Germany.

The classic feature of this game is that a player can win at any time if they pot the 9-ball, as long as they first hit the designated object ball (which players must hit in numerical order). The nine balls are placed in a diamond-figured configuration, with the 1-ball positioned at the front and the 9-ball in the center.

In much of Europe and the Commonwealth, the most common form of the game is eight-ball pool, although it is still played widely across America too.

This game is played with seven stripes and seven solids, and a black 8-ball. The balls are racked in a triangle formation, with the

1920

Nine-ball pool is widely known as a newer form of the game, but it already dates back nearly a century, with the first game reported to have been played in the United States.

8-ball placed behind the front three balls. A player must clear his particular set of balls from the table before potting the 8-ball for victory.

In Britain, and other countries in the Commonwealth, you will see the game of blackball played, which is an internationally recognized variant of eight-ball. In this game, red and yellow balls are used instead of stripes and solids.

Coin-operated tables in pool halls and bars are commonplace, with the balls captured inside the table when potted, and only the cue ball returned (when accidentally potted).

Pool has clearly been a great success story overall, but one can't help feeling that when you consider the widespread popularity of the game, it could sell itself even better than it does. The game lends itself very well to television coverage. In the US, nine-ball is the most popular form of the game on TV, perhaps because of the fast pace and the excitement of the use of English, jump shots, and power shots.

The major pool tournaments can attract big crowds, with spectators often creating a superb atmosphere. The top players thrive off this, and the crowds can often inspire them to even greater heights.

The Future of Pool

Pool will always be seen first and foremost as a bar game, but that shouldn't preclude it from an even wider profile than it enjoys. I have already mentioned the success of snooker, a sport that has probably enjoyed its very best days in Europe, but which continues to boom in the Far East, where tens of millions tune in to watch on television.

The bar sport darts has shaken off its old-fashioned image around the world and big tournaments now attract huge crowds, with the venues glitzy and the atmosphere raucous. And you can barely switch on your television these days

without seeing a game of darts being played.

All this should give pool confidence in its future, especially when you consider how many people are actually aware of the game. It does sometimes make you wonder why the sport hasn't pushed itself even more vigorously toward gaining a higher profile. Maybe there has simply been too much politics at play—there have historically been too many rules and too many governing organizations.

But this book is not necessarily aimed toward the game at the highest level, but rather at those who simply enjoy playing. As mentioned, a person's background is irrelevant when playing this game. Whatever one's economic, social, or cultural status, we are all equal when playing pool—it is a fine leveler. People may not even always know all the proper rules, but they simply love playing the game.

There is only one absolute certainty when you talk about this great game—whatever the new attractions on offer in this changing world, pool is here to stay. And it is here to stay for many years and generations to come.

Many major pool tournaments are screened on television, but some professionals believe there is room for the game to be aired more than it is.

Chapter Two: TOOLS OF THE TRADE

Without the proper equipment you won't have much chance of succeeding in the game. So what should you look for in the pool table and cue? And what should you do to make sure your equipment is properly maintained?

From the color of the chalk you use, down to the nap of the table you play on, there are many factors that can affect the quality of your game. Choosing the right equipment and making sure it is properly maintained is a must for anyone who is serious about playing pool.

The Table

It hardly needs to be explained that in order to give yourself the best chance of success in the game, the equipment that you play with needs to be of the best possible quality. We've all seen poorly maintained tables—with scratches on the wood, holes in the cloth, and dirt all over them. This shouldn't really be the case in most pool halls, which cater solely for the game, but in your average bar they are often to be seen.

Proportionally, the size of a table is usually half as wide as it is long. Generally speaking, tables measure 9 ft by 4½ ft in the nine-ball game, and this is certainly the case in professional tournaments. Many eight-ball tables, particularly those in Europe but also across America, measure 7 ft by 3½ ft. This is the classic size of table that you will play on in a bar, and is known as a "bar box." You may come across a number of other sizes in use as well, with the smallest tending to be 6 ft by 3 ft.

The playing surface of the table, known as the bed, is usually made of slate. Tables are covered in a green or blue

wool cloth, or sometimes a wool/nylon combination, which is known as baize.

CHOOSING A TABLE

For people who are thinking of buying a pool table or have one on their premises, there are some basic points to follow.

You should generally avoid tables with composition wood beds; these are prone to warp in damp conditions.

You should check that the rails are screwed into position and not glued. Ascertain whether the cloth covering the table is made from a natural fiber (with nap) or man-made fiber (napless). The table bed size should be approximately twice as long as it is wide, and the pockets should be all the same size.

Probably the most important aspect is the bed of the table and quality of the cloth, and you should check that the balls run straight and true. American tables tend not to

have a nap, but some still do, and in other parts of the world most tables will have one. If there is a nap, it runs from the head area (the D end) of the table to the foot rail (see page 33). It is basically a directional pile created by the short fuzzy ends of fibers on the surface cloth that project upward from the lie. The nap can create a favorable and unfavorable direction for rolling balls.

Running the flat of your hand over the table by the rails will highlight any damage. The

Generally speaking, the smoother the nap is, the faster the table will play. Learning to play according to the nap is a genuine skill.

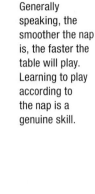

legs should have adjusters to compensate for uneven floors. There are few things more frustrating than the balls gravitating toward a particular side of the table, potentially spoiling a game. If the table has fold-away legs, you should make sure that they are properly hinged and are strong enough to prevent the table from moving during play.

Owning your own pool table is by no means an impossible dream, and if looked after properly it can give you many years of pleasure. The advice for buying a table could really apply to any purchase that you make, and boils down to common sense. Usually it isn't sensible to opt for the cheapest table, but rather one that has been made by a reputable manufacturer. If a new table is out of your price range, ask a manufacturer if they supply reconditioned tables.

HOW BIG?

In terms of size, it would probably be best not to look at anything smaller than 6 ft by 3 ft. Any game on a table smaller than that would more than likely lack real substance. Of course one of the major considerations is the space available for accommodating the table. The normal requirement for space around the table is 4 feet. Most of us have played in places where you're raising your cue to play a shot due to a lack of space. It doesn't really make for a fair or serious contest.

It should be said that pool does owe some of its success to the skill of manufacturers. Part of the reason for the spread of the game worldwide is the farsightedness of these people, and new tables made today are known for their excellent quality. Such is the popularity of the game that many thousands of new tables are bought every year.

Jordan Church

**Twice World Junior Eight-Ball Champion
and England International**

Playing a shot

When you are playing any shot, you should make sure your head is completely still. This should ensure that the rest of your body is still, which is essential if you want the desired outcome. It will always be useful when you are first starting out to get somebody to stand next to you to make sure that you are holding the cue in the right place as soon as the tip touches the white ball. You should soon come to realize that the process is all about timing. When organizing the bridge hand, don't be afraid to start out gradually, spreading your fingers slowly and then lifting up the middle of your hand. Your thumb should be pushed as high up to your knuckle as possible. You should never feel overly rushed when playing a shot, particularly when starting out.

Accuracy is important when playing a shot, so take your time.

The Table

31

Sizes and Markings

As already mentioned, the classic sizes of table are 9 ft by 4½ ft, and 7 ft by 3½ ft, although there are plenty of tables measuring 8 ft by 4 ft in operation as well. As a general rule, the smaller tables are used in eight-ball or blackball pool, and are particularly common in Commonwealth countries, like Great Britain and Australia. The larger tables, measuring 9 ft by 4½ ft, are the classic size used in nine-ball pool, and there will be many games taking place on this type across America as you read this. As well as the tables being bigger, the sizes of the pockets are noticeably larger as well. On the smaller tables, the pockets tend to be tighter, making potting balls more of a challenge.

The marks opposite indicate various (invisible) string lines bisecting the table. The head spot is at the center of a

1470
King Louis XI of France is the first recorded owner of a table. It is understood that the table had no pockets, but did have a hole in the middle.

line which is known as the head string. The number 6 indicates the head string, with the area above this on the table referred to as the head area, or the kitchen. The foot spot is at the center of the line indicated by the number 2. This line is known as the foot string.

On some eight-ball tables, certainly in Commonwealth countries, there will be a D on the head string. You will play the initial shot of every game, the break shot, from this part of the table.

At the highest level of the game, the World Pool-Billiard Association states that the table must be made of slate that is no less than 1 inch thick. It is likely that the slate is often less thick than this on tables in many bars and pools halls.

On the bigger tables, you will often see markings at regular intervals on the rails. If you have wondered about their use, the marks are there to help the player accurately calculate the angle a ball will rebound at when played as a natural shot.

FOOT RAIL

1

FOOT SPOT

SIDE RAIL

2

FOOT STRING

3

LONG STRING

4

5

HEAD SPOT

6

HEAD STRING

HEAD AREA

7

HEAD RAIL

Maintenance

Taking good care to maintain a table is crucial. If there is a nap on the table, the cloth should be regularly brushed (in the direction of the nap) to remove chalk marks, both on the bed and rails. Chalk that is not brushed away could easily creep into the weave and ruin the nap. If possible, the table should be covered when not in use—this will help greatly in its general maintenance.

The placement of a table can be extremely important.

If possible, it should not be placed in a position where it is constantly exposed to sunlight. The cloth will undoubtedly fade over time, and sun can also bleach the table's finish. If it is necessary to put a pool table near to a window, it would be sensible to consider purchasing a blind to be used during daylight hours.

The cloth will naturally show some signs of wear and tear over a period of time. If it does show these signs, it would be advisable to use a table iron on it, making sure that any fluff is removed from the surface first. Or, ask an expert to re-stretch the cloth.

For spots that are wearing off on the table, a small dot or cross should be applied with a felt pen, rather than using self-adhesive spots. These can leave a nasty mark on the

Test out the table with a few practice shots to ensure it is playing properly.

cloth that is extremely difficult to remove. When choosing chalk, make sure it is not too abrasive, and that the color of chalk matches the color of the cloth. Blue and green chalks are readily available.

Although keeping the cloth in good order is probably the top priority, it is also wise to maintain the quality of the wood (or leather, as will sometimes be found round the pockets). A classic furniture oil or polish will keep these areas looking in good shape and, more importantly, lasting longer.

It is always sensible to check that the table is level. A long spirit level could be used to ensure this is the case.

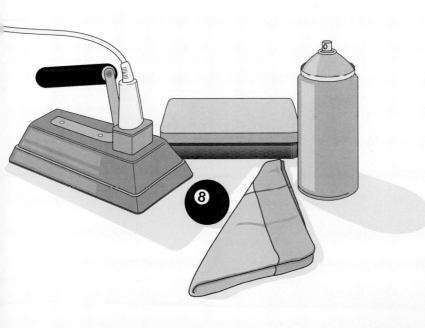

Balls

Where would we be without our balls? As is the case with so many of the world's great sports, they are essential in pool.

The earliest balls were made of wood and then clay, before ivory was used for many hundreds of years. In 1869 the American inventor John Wesley Hyatt invented a composition material for billiard balls called nitrocellulose, and a year later this was commercially branded as Celluloid, the first industrial plastic. Unfortunately the Celluloid was volatile in production, making it impractical. Various other synthetic materials for balls were then experimented with, including Bakelite and Crystalate. And today the balls are generally made of phenolic resin. The most famous brand names are probably Aramith and Brunswick Centennial. Other plastics and resins such as polyester and clear acrylic are also sometimes used. New balls made today are of excellent quality and if looked after properly can last for many years.

SIZES

As with most aspects of the game there is little in the way of uniformity, and pool balls come in different sizes.

The balls measure 2¼ inches in diameter. In nine-ball, the cue balls in a set can often be larger or denser, to make it easier for the return mechanism inside the table to separate

1837
John Wesley Hyatt, the inventor of the nitrocellulose billiard ball, is born in New York, and by the age of 16 he begins working as a printer. Among his many inventions is the multiple-stitch sewing machine.

it from object balls and return it during a game.

With eight-ball pool, the cue ball will often be ⅛ inch smaller, again allowing it to take a different route through a coin-operated table when accidentally potted. You will on occasion today see a cue ball that is the same size as the other balls, but it can still be separated from the rest of the balls due to its iron content, by magnets fitted inside the table.

COLORS

The white ball is a regular theme of the different kinds of pool, but the balls can otherwise differ. Stripes and solids are used in classic eight-ball pool, while in the game of blackball, red and yellow balls are used.

Urban legend has it that Celluloid balls would sometimes explode during a game.

As with any other equipment used in the game, it is important that the balls are properly maintained. They should be regularly inspected for any damage. If a ball is cracked or pitted, it should be changed. If the balls look dull, a damp cloth can be used to polish them. It is surprising how much these simple actions can help to improve a game. Pool is best played when the balls sport a fine sheen because this reduces their friction on the cloth and makes them play truer.

It is important to ensure that there isn't any chalk or dirt left on the balls. If there is, the chance of a player suffering from poor contact is increased. The word "cling" is widely used to describe unexpectedly poor contact between the cue ball and object ball, something that has been cursed by generations of people that have played cue sports.

Either the cue ball or object ball, or both, are liable to jump in the air. At worst a pot will be missed, while at best a ball will be potted but without decent position for the next shot. It is possible that this could be caused by static electricity, but if there is any dirt or chalk on a ball this could also be the reason.

If you play the game for fun, you will probably have been involved in many games where balls have flown off the table by accident. If the balls are of decent quality, this shouldn't really affect them, no matter what kind of floor they fall onto. It is still worth checking them straight after however, to make sure they haven't been obviously damaged in any way.

Maintenance

The table should be brushed every day after use if you want to keep it in top condition. If the table has a nap you should brush down the table from the head area. A useful tip is to use a damp cloth five minutes after brushing, which will pick up the dust that has settled on the cloth. After that you can use the iron, and this should ensure the table keeps its speed. The balls should be cleaned once a week, first with a wet cloth and then with a dry cloth. Some people use polish, but this is generally a mistake as it will result in the balls picking up dirt.

Carefully chalk your cue tip and avoid getting excess chalk on the edges of the cue. Brush any chalk off the table to maintain its condition.

Balls

The Cue

The importance of the cue cannot be underestimated. For players at the top of the game, their favorite cue is an essential tool. If that cue is damaged or lost, the effect on a player can be truly devastating.

In fact even players who play for fun, but want to improve their game, often own their own cue. As someone that has battled with the game using some of the awful cues that you sometimes find in bars, I can appreciate the value of splashing cash on a decent cue. We have all seen and used the implements I have talked about; with chipped wood and huge flat tips, they are often far too short for serious play.

Cues are generally made from two types of wood, with maple being the most common. The top end is turned from a straight-grained wood, tapered down to about ⅝ inch, and then spliced to a darker, heavier wood that gives the cue its weight. Traditional, and more expensive, cues are made from one complete piece of wood with a weight added in a recess at the butt end. The cheaper club cue is normally made from ramin but this type is liable to warp and fracture as the wood tends to be brittle.

The two-part (or even four-part) cue is designed to be easy to carry, and will come with a case. Most cues are around 57 or 58 inches long, and although the weight varies considerably, most weigh between 17 and 21 ounces.

When choosing a cue, you should, first and foremost, check that it is straight. A simple way to check this is to lay the cue on a flat surface and roll it. With cues that come in different sections, check that the joints screw up flush and firm. The grain should run the full length of the cue.

The choice of the tip end can be quite contentious. Some players prefer the screw-in type, while others swear by the complete slot-on molded type or the glue-on type. The tip can be supplied coated in varnish or smooth from molding, and will need roughening up to take the chalk. The tip should be evenly rounded to enable it to make positive contact with the cue ball and may need gently filing down at first. The state of the tip should be checked before, and during, a game.

A decent pool cue is essential for a good game. It makes sense to invest in a high-quality instrument if you are someone who is frustrated by the damaged and often poor-quality cues found in bars.

Caring for Your Cue

A cue should be looked after at all times. It should be stored upright in a case, and never left in direct sunlight or extreme temperatures. A damp cloth can be used to keep the cue clean, wiping away any chalk marks or other dirt.

A cue can be personally made to suit the height and weight of a player, and professional players will nearly always have one made to suit their particular requirements. When cues are handmade, only the highest quality woods are used, which are straight-grained and fully matured. The cue begins its life as a sawn rectangular "blank." The grain is checked to make sure it runs straight down the length. Next, the maker can begin a series of hand operations that finally achieves the taper, indentifying the handmade cue from the rest. The blank is planed down in several operations and allowed to settle between each stage. Distortion at any stage will result in the blank being discarded.

After the final planing, each shaft is checked for balance, rigidity, and straightness before being cut to the appropriate length. The butt gives the cue its weight and balance. It is shaped and then joined to the shaft with a handmade fishtail splice.

This system allows the two woods to weld as one

1675

Players use the mace, which has a flat end used for shoving the ball, but it is reported in this year that they begin to hit balls with the tail end. The way is being paved for the development of the cue.

If you are serious about improving your game, you don't need to wait and save up forever to afford a decent cue. You can still pick up a very good one today for around $150. Owning your own cue can instantly make you feel more serious about the game.

and allows the gentlest cue action to feel the contact of cue tip to cue ball. A brass ferrule is fixed to the tip of the cue to protect the grain from damage, and then the cue tip is added.

The whole cue is inspected for quality. Only then will it be converted to a two-piece (or more). The screw joints are precision made and, when fitted, allow the grain to run naturally the length of the shaft. Cues selected for production undergo a number of sandings with different grades of abrasive, and are then polished with linseed oil to give a silk-like action. The butt is burnished and then waxed.

The Cue Tip

The contact of the cue tip on the cue ball will always be made more positive by chalking the tip. The method of putting chalk on the cue tip is simple, but still vitally important to get right. The chalk should ideally be applied across the tip two or three times, rotating the cue at the same time.

If the tip still looks like it needs more chalk, more can be added using the same gentle method. Any surplus chalk can be removed by gently tapping the cue. At the same time, the cue tip should be inspected for any damage or misshape. It is important to keep a close eye on your chalk cube as well, and if there doesn't seem to be enough chalk it is time to purchase a new cube. It will be handy to keep a spare one, especially if you are playing in a competition.

Chalking the tip of the cue increases friction between the cue and the cue ball, reducing slippage.

It is straight-forward to have your cue re-tipped professionally, but it is also quite easy to do yourself by following the guidelines below.

REPLACING A TIP

If re-tipping is required, many pool clubs will offer this service, but you can do it yourself if you follow the correct guidelines. First ensure that the purchased tip is in good condition, and slightly bigger than the diameter of the end of the cue.

Generally speaking, the old tip can be cut off with a sharp knife and its remains carefully filed off using sandpaper. A new tip can be attached to the cue using glue, with superglue most likely to do the job effectively. The new tip can then be modeled down to the desired shape, again using sandpaper. Any good player will tell you how important it is to feel comfortable with your tip, allowing you to concentrate and fully focus on the shot at hand.

Chapter Three:
BACK TO BASICS

The basics need to be mastered in any game, and in pool it is essential that you play your shots in the correct fashion. But how are you supposed to stand when playing, and how should you hold the cue? And how should you practice using the basic skills?

This chapter goes through the essential techniques required to master the game of pool. From basic stance to more advanced shots, the majority of your game will be based on the tips and explanations contained in the following pages.

Learning the Skills

Pool can sometimes look like an incredibly simple game to play, particularly if you are watching the top players compete in tournaments on television. On occasion, this can be infuriating, particularly if you are just starting to play the game or you seriously want to improve your skills. But you could do a lot worse than watching, and studying, the top players in action. Their games are characterized by skillful cue-work, careful planning, and clever tactics. They seem to be able to make clearances from nothing, potting balls from seemingly impossible angles. What should always be remembered is that

Before you can worry about the complex shots and tactics involved in playing the game, you have to make sure that you are giving yourself the best chance of success by establishing whether those basics are properly in place.

professional players practice for six or seven hours a day, sometimes more. Their skills didn't materialize as if by magic; they are carefully honed and developed. It may be one of life's great clichés, but also one of its great truths: practice really can make perfect.

As is the case if you are playing any sport, it is important first and foremost to get the basics right. Are you holding the cue properly? Are you positioning yourself correctly to play the shot? Is your bridge hand in the right place? As with many problems, these seemingly simple matters can appear insurmountable at first, but we've all started at the beginning at one time or another.

Stance

All good players know they must stand firm and balanced, with no obvious body movement that can spoil the shot. In fact the only movement that needs to be made is the cue action. This should be smooth, coming from the shoulder and elbow joints.

Presuming that you are right-handed (and obviously doing the opposite if left-handed) a good exercise is to place the cue ball on the head spot, where you would play the break shot from. The left hand should be placed on the table, and the cue picked up by the right hand.

You should bend at the waist and move back, keeping the cue parallel to the table. As you move back, your weight will naturally be thrown forward and taken by the hand resting on the table. Your right arm should be held tight to the body, swinging it back as the body is bent. You should then

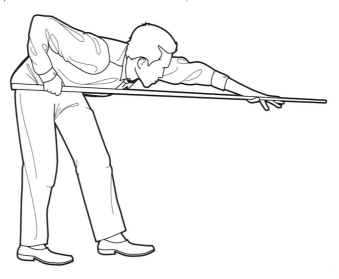

move back until you can feel your lower right arm making a right-angle with the cue.

Your feet should be around 8 inches apart, with the left leg moved forward slightly and bent at the knee. The right leg should remain straight, and foot twisted slightly out of line. At this point your head should be moved forward, but kept upright.

As you look down the table to the shot, you should check that the cue ball, the middle of your head, shoulder, and back arm are all in a straight line. Your chin should not be more than around 12 inches from the cue. It is important not to stand too erect, aiming the cue as accurately as possible. The right arm should be tucked tight into the body, helping to ensure that the cue action is as smooth and straight as possible.

A good initial exercise to check whether your stance is firm enough is to ask a friend to give you a gentle push on the shoulders. If you wobble, even slightly, this is a clear indication that something about your stance isn't right and needs additional work.

Preparing for a Shot

Generally speaking, aiming the cue is a subconscious action, with the brain already having processed where the balls are on the table, and which one you are going to hit. Indeed, an experienced player will not only have processed their next shot, but the one after that, and sometimes three or four shots down the line. But let's not stray too far from the basics.

You should stand behind the line of the shot before taking your stance, rather than arriving at it from the side. Sometimes you might see a talented player going down to play their shot quickly, from a more upright position. The most appropriate word to sum up this approach would probably be complacency, and it should be discouraged, because as with any sport bad habits can soon be picked up and become commonplace, particularly if playing the game regularly.

Often you may find that the shoulder isn't quite in the right position, or your elbow is sticking out. Even the slightest imperfection in stance can

1680

Simonis, the company that produces cloth used on pool tables, sets up its first factory in the town of Verviers, Belgium. The name Iwan Simonis has become synonymous with pool, and all cue sports.

affect the quality of your shot. Again it is important to check that everything is in line as you prepare to hit the cue ball. Once you manage to establish a proper stance, you can begin to think about the right shot to play.

If you begin to think that you might have cracked the stance, this is never a bad time to ask a friend to conduct the same initial experiment again, to give your shoulders a slight push. If you find there is no wobbling, and you remain straight, the chances are that you really are on your way. When you are happy with how you are positioned to play, you can begin to think about actually playing a shot.

In the game of golf, much is made of a player's swing; where they are standing, and the position of their body. It is just as important in pool, and the key to it is feeling totally natural in your position when playing a shot.

Holding the Cue

The next aspect of the game you should focus on is how you hold the cue. It should be remembered that the cue is a light, precision piece of worked wood, although some of the cues that are found in bars across the world would struggle to fit that description. But let's presume that we are working with a proper cue.

Ideally, the cue should be held around 2 inches from the butt end (though this can differ according to your height), with a firm grip at first. It is important to feel comfortable with the cue in hand. The grip should then be relaxed, and your fingers curled around the wood.

The cue should be gripped in the arc of your thumb and first finger, with the other fingers wrapped around and adding enough pressure to hold the cue against your palm. Most of the weight should be taken by your thumb, first finger, and middle finger.

An overly firm or tight grip can stiffen your wrist, impeding the swing and

Jordan Church

Grip

Where you hold the cue will depend on the length of your arms and your height, but when the tip of the cue strikes the cue ball, your back arm should be at ninety degrees so that your timing is right. You shouldn't grip the cue too tightly.

dulling the "feel" of the shot. It can be much more difficult to follow the shot through properly if this is the case. A light grip gives you that feel, allowing you to control the contact of the cue and cue ball more accurately, and also giving your wrist enough movement to follow the swing of the arm when playing the shot.

Sometimes the grip a player uses can depend on the shot they are attempting to play. If the shot requires a gentle touch, it can be useful to grip the cue with your fingertips, rather than wrapping your hand around. For a shot that requires more power, a firmer grip is more appropriate, but the cue should still not be held tightly.

A good experiment would be to hold a packet of butter with the same grip as you would a pool cue. If you start to feel your fingers and hand making an impression on the butter, it is a sign that your grip is too tight.

Holding the Cue

Common Faults

One problem that some players develop is putting their thumb in the wrong position, resting it in a straight position on the cue. The thumb should be wrapped around the cue with the fingers.

It is also important that the wrist is in a straight line with the arm. If it is turned too far in either direction, this can have a damaging effect on the shot. If your wrist is in the wrong position, this could easily lead to your elbow being placed in the wrong position also.

One of the best tests to determine whether you are holding the cue correctly is to see whether you are comfortable playing the shot. If anything feels unnatural the chances are that your fingers or thumb are in the wrong place, your wrist isn't straight, or you are holding the cue too tightly.

Admittedly it is sometimes tempting to hold the cue tightly, gripping it for dear life, as if this will somehow improve the quality of your shot and game. Newcomers can be easily forgiven for adopting this approach. This should always be discouraged, however, as a lighter grip will in time produce the best results. The muscles in the arm will be more relaxed when the grip is loosened, allowing much greater control over the shot.

At first you should try moving the cue back and forth without playing a shot, to determine whether the process seems natural. Again it would be useful to try and watch footage of the top players in action. Their action will be extremely smooth, but is founded on these same basic principles.

As with any part of your game, the more you play, the greater confidence you will have in how you hold the cue. Practice should make you realize that your grip doesn't need to be tight to be successful.

The Bridge Hand

We have determined that the way you hold the cue is crucial, but equally important is how you arrange your other hand. One won't work properly without the other. Now I've seen all manner of hugely awkward bridge hands on my travels, and I think it's fair to say that when any of us start playing, it is one of the most difficult aspects of the game to get right. Again the simple principle is that if you are fully comfortable when playing a shot, the chances are that you are heading in the right direction.

When forming the bridge, you should lay the palm of your hand flat on the table, and then spread your fingers apart. Ideally you should place this hand between 6 and 10 inches away from the cue ball. When beginning, many players prefer being nearer the cue ball, often more as a source of comfort than anything else, but soon learn to move the hand farther back.

You should raise your hand with your fingers still on the cloth and evenly spaced apart. When pressing down gently on your hand, you should feel that your grip on the cloth is tightening. If you then raise your thumb and press it forward into the side of your first finger, your hand will now be bent and slightly fixed. The normal stance should be adopted to play a shot and the cue gripped correctly.

The cue should then be laid in the "V" between your thumb and first finger, adjusting the height of your bridge to allow you to play the ball as you want it, while keeping your cue parallel to the table.

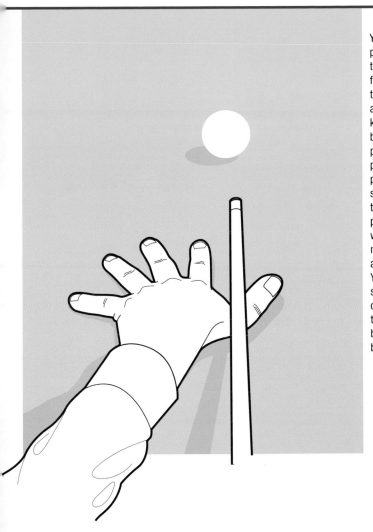

You may see a player wrapping their thumb and first finger around the cue, making a hole. This is known as a closed bridge. Many players, including professionals, prefer the greater stability that this can provide, particularly when playing more powerful or advanced shots. You should make sure that you are comfortable with the more regular bridge hand before trying this.

More Advanced Techniques

When you become more proficient at the game, and want to try controlling the cue ball, you may find it is necessary to move the bridge hand farther away from the target. This makes it possible to take a longer backswing, giving you a better chance of moving the cue ball as you intend.

When using power it is also sensible to give yourself a longer swing with your cue action, again moving the bridge hand farther back. When the shot requires a particular degree of accuracy, or needs to be hit softly, it will be better to move the hand closer to the ball.

The bridge hand should be flexible, and if positioned properly it will be. It should be easy enough to move the hand if necessary for certain more difficult shots—which will include putting spin on the ball. You should feel comfortable enough to lift the palm higher off the table, raising your knuckles, where appropriate.

Also, it isn't always the case that you are left with ideal cueing during a game of pool. Sometimes you will need to be cueing directly over another ball to hit the cue ball. Again you should rely on the flexibility of your bridge hand, if necessary raising your fingers to an almost upright position.

Even in this position, you should still be able to create

a "V" between your thumb and first finger, through which the cue can fit nicely. When the cue ball is near or stuck against a rail, it is easy to become disheartened as this means you won't face an easy shot, but a good solid bridge hand can be a major help.

The same principles can be applied, making sure the hand is comfortable and flexible while resting on the rail. Depending on the size of the rail, and they do differ, it may be necessary to keep your thumb hanging behind the rail. If this is the case, it could be more comfortable to move the index finger and play the shot between index finger and middle fingers. When playing a shot in more normal conditions it is nearly always best to play the shot in the "V" between thumb and index finger. Sometimes, when the cue ball is stuck against a rail, it might feel more comfortable to raise your bridge hand, with your fingers upright, allowing you to strike down on the ball.

Many people can struggle with their bridge hand at first, mainly because it doesn't feel at all natural. In time, however, the process should become second nature, something you do on auto-pilot.

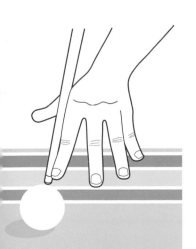

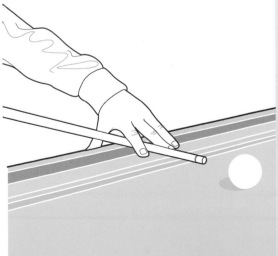

Cue Action

So you're standing in the right position, you're holding the cue in the right way, and your bridge hand is perfectly placed. What could possibly go wrong from here? Well, the most important part is clearly still to come, and that is playing the shot.

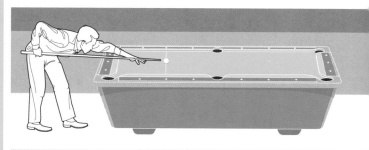

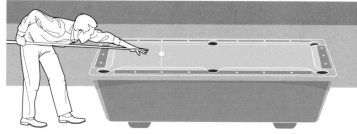

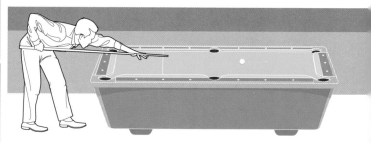

You should carefully place the cue in the "V" of the bridge, and aim toward the direction of the shot. It is advisable to swing your cue back and forth three or four times to make sure you are feeling comfortable with your stance and grip.

The cue should be swung back until it is almost under your shoulder. You should pause if necessary and check the direction of the cue, making sure everything is in line and as smooth as possible.

Only your cueing arm should be moving at this stage, with the rest of your body still. When you are ready to take your shot, you should move the cue back a few inches from the ball. This will depend on the type of shot being played. If you are playing a more gentle shot, you should move the cue nearer to the ball.

You should be focusing on the cue ball and object ball, moving your eyes to both, ensuring that you know where you are aiming. As the shot approaches, your attention should focus on the object ball. You should then make your final swing, bringing the tip of the cue into contact with the cue ball.

When playing the shot, you should make sure that you continue the swing forward, past the point of impact, and stop a few inches beyond the position of the cue ball. Your forearm, which has been used to play the shot, should meet your upper arm, which has been still and straight, supporting your bridge hand. This simple process needs to feel comfortable, since it will be repeated many thousands of times in the lifetime of a pool player.

Let's face it, no two players are identical. Some take their shots very quickly, but others prefer to take much longer, with more time for preparation.

Practice Makes Perfect

It may take a long time to learn how to hit the cue ball properly, and at the right pace, but this is essential.

The accuracy of each shot depends on good direction and pace. You can experiment with pace at any time, providing you can find a table to practice on. I can't imagine you would be the most popular person in the world if you frequented the one table in a local bar for hours on end, but if you're not lucky enough to have a pool table at home there are numerous pool halls you could play in to help improve your game.

You can try a few simple experiments, using just the cue ball and one object ball. Try playing a shot using light pace, so that the object ball travels a few inches only.

Remember that you can alter your bridge hand to facilitate the playing of any shot, and for a gentle shot it would be advisable to move it closer to the ball.

Practice simple shots when starting out.

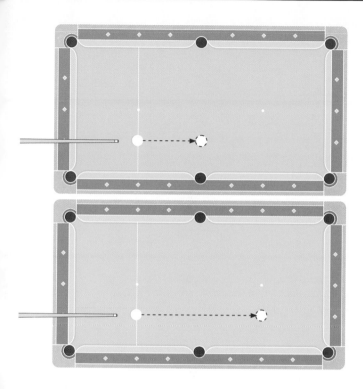

With the first shot you should place the cue ball on the head string, or baulk line. The cue ball should be hit with light pace, just enough for it to reach the center of the table. The second shot, with the cue ball placed to the right of center, will give you practice with using stronger pace. Try and hit the shot with enough pace to leave the cue ball on the foot string.

A shot with light pace should move the object ball to just short of the position the cue ball would have stopped at when played with a straight shot. You can slowly increase the power of the shot, playing the ball at a more medium pace.

If there are spots on the side of the table, this will help you to aim for a particular place on the table. If not, it should be easy enough to imagine a spot. You could aim to hit the object ball toward the foot spot, or to land near a rail.

Working with the Rails

The rails can provide the most useful of tools in these exercises. If you want to increase the power of your shot still further, you could aim to strike the cue ball against a rail and for it to bounce back and finish in a particular spot.

A simple yet effective method could be to hit the ball from the center of the table and aim to bounce it off the foot rail. You should try hitting the cue ball with sufficient pace for it to rebound off the rail and bounce back toward the center of the table.

As well as playing the shot straight up and down the table, you could try playing it with a slight angle, starting the ball from the right-hand side of the table and aiming toward the middle of the foot rail so the ball will eventually finish on the left-hand side of the table. As much as anything else, you will be giving yourself some idea of how balls react when they bounce off the rails, and this will be an important factor in any game of pool.

HITTING HARD

Now we all need to play powerful shots when the occasion demands. So in time, when you are more comfortable with hitting the cue ball with some degree of accuracy, you would be well advised to practice some more powerful shots. Again, you might want to use the same exercise as before, but this time trying to hit the

1829

The two-piece cue is first used in this year—this was an important development, with the cues designed to make them much easier to carry and use.

ball against both the foot rail and head rail. You might want to aim for the ball to finish somewhere around the center of the table.

In truth, you would be unlikely to need shots requiring these levels of power in a game very often, apart from perhaps the break shot. You may find that you miscue a few times at first, because it will take some time to get used to hitting the ball hard. In time you should find that you are cueing more smoothly, and if you are starting to get somewhere near with your attempts, there can be little doubt that you are moving in the right direction.

Using the rails for an angle shot is simple and effective.

Mastering the Basics

While you are practicing these exercises, you should be aiming to hit the center of the cue ball. You should also be aiming to strike the object ball "full in the face," that is to say in the center and not either side of the ball. This is the simplest and most basic way of hitting the cue ball.

It should almost go without saying that if you find yourself struggling with these exercises you can go back to the beginning if necessary. Check that you are holding the cue in the correct fashion and that it feels comfortable. Make sure the bridge hand is properly resting on the table and providing you with a "V" for the cue to slide through nicely. Maybe you are bent too far over, with your body not in line with the shot.

Even though chalk will be absolutely necessary for more complex shots, it is also good practice at this point to make sure it is applied properly across the tip.

By applying chalk you are increasing the tips friction, enabling an accurate shot.

Gospel according to...
Jordan Church

Practice

You should practice parts of your game that you think need working on. If your break isn't working very well, you should spend time playing that shot a dozen times or more. If you find potting balls along a cushion difficult, you should practice this shot. Generally speaking, good potting is the key to success, so line up three or four balls in a certain part of the table and try to pot them in succession. If I have missed a particular shot in a match, I will spend time mastering this shot in practice. In a sense it can seem like you are punishing yourself by reliving a disappointing moment, but this is a good way to improve your game. You should always treat practice seriously, making sure there are no distractions—as if you were playing in an important match.

Practice and perseverance are essential for improving your game.

Mastering the Basics

69

Potting

There are few better feelings in pool than sinking a ball in a pocket (known as "potting a ball"). It's what we're all in this game for. When practicing it would be sensible to first line up a natural shot, the kind we all dream of facing to beat our opponent and win a match. You should align the cue ball and object ball to a pocket. At first, you might want to place the object ball near a pocket, and then gradually move it farther away if you are potting with ease.

Firstly, line the object ball up to pot it into a center pocket. You may find that the cue ball sometimes

If you play on different tables, you will notice a difference.

Tables can vary in size, some pockets can be tighter than others, and certain cloths can make the balls move at different speeds, particularly if they have a nap. Sometimes the balls can bounce powerfully off a rail, while at other times they can be slowed down significantly. Whatever table you play on, as long as you are following the basics, you are giving yourself the best possible chance of success.

follows the object ball into the pocket. This is natural when you first begin, largely because you are not attempting to control the cue ball in any serious way.

In time, start attempting to pot the balls in the corner pockets. Again you can move the balls farther apart if necessary, giving yourself a chance to practice a more powerful shot.

When you are feeling confident that you can aim with accuracy and pot the object ball, you can move on and try to pot balls that aren't in a natural line with the pocket. To play shots at an angle, you will need to hit a certain part of the cue ball away from the center, which will be a very useful gauge of the quality of your cueing and accuracy of your shots.

Attempting Angles

Learning to cue at an angle to the object ball and moving it in a direction away from the impact point isn't easy, and won't be grasped overnight. Determining the angle of deflection is not a skill players are born with, nor is it a matter of simple mathematics. The angle of deflection at which the object ball travels after impact is governed by the angle both of the line of play and the pace.

Angle shots can sometimes appear to be almost impossible to execute, but that won't necessarily be the case. The size of the pockets can sometimes be generous enough to give the ball half a chance of dropping, but the balls still need to be hit in the right place. The exercises already outlined in this chapter involved hitting the object ball in the center—a full-face contact—but now you will have to aim at a different part of the object ball. A three-quarter face contact, or three-quarter ball, will connect with the object ball slightly to the left or right of full in the face, and will move that object ball between 5 and 30 degrees. A half-face contact will move the object ball between 30 and 60 degrees, while a quarter-face contact, which will be a much thinner contact with the object ball, will move it between 60 and 80 degrees.

Often you will find, during an average game, that a cut shot will be required when attempting to pot a ball into a center pocket, so that would

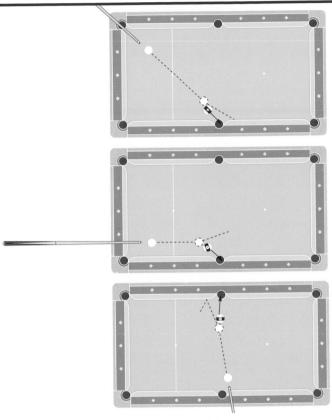

You should practice making contact with an object ball at different angles. You should first line up a cue ball and object ball so that they are in almost a direct line with a pocket. This will give you good initial practice and is a good gauge of how to judge angles. As you become more confident, you should place the balls in such a way that you will need to make half-face, or quarter-face, contact with the object ball in order to pot it.

be a useful place to start practicing. You could line up a ball near the center pocket, and begin by attempting to play a three-quarter face shot. This will only differ slightly from a straight shot, and will ease you into angled shots as gently as possible.

You could try to strike the ball with a half-face contact soon after; a shot that usually requires more pace. A quarter-face contact needs even more skill, and will probably take longer to master.

The Fine Cut

The fine cut is the most difficult shot to play when hitting an object ball at an angle, and even experienced players will be all too aware of how easy it is for this shot to go wrong. This is often due to the fact that you need to play the ball at some pace to execute the shot properly, sometimes with such power that you can never be totally sure of how the cue ball will behave.

The object ball should move almost at right angles. Your eyes must be focused on the extreme edge of the object ball as you attempt to play the shot. Try cutting the ball into the center pockets first, and then the corner pockets, with the same principles to be applied for both.

If you went to watch a player in a very good local league, or even semi-serious bar competition, you would sometimes see the object ball missed completely when attempting a fine cut.

Generally speaking, you may also find that the cue ball flies into a pocket when attempting a fine cut. Again, this is to be expected, and will largely be because you have been focusing on striking the object ball, not controlling the cue ball.

The next exercise you might want to try is to learn how to use the rails to your advantage. Again there is no mathematical science behind how the balls react and behave when bouncing off the rail. While it can be difficult to get to grips with at first, you should try to see the rails as an ally. Becoming proficient at using the rails can provide a major boost to the quality of your game.

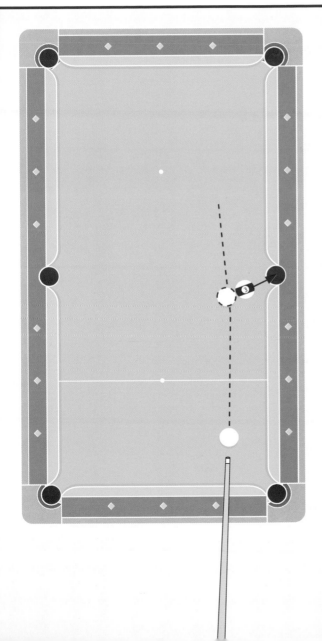

Don't become frustrated if you miss the ball completely—this is understandable and perfectly normal. In fact, it is sometimes a better sign if you narrowly miss the ball than if you strike it full in the face when attempting a fine cut.

The Bank Shot

On many occasions you will be faced with needing to pot a bank shot, which is referred to as a double in many countries, including Britain. This simply means hitting the object ball against a rail, in such a way that it will bounce back and fall into the opposite pocket. This will invariably be a shot that you will play into the center pockets.

Before worrying about trying to execute a bank shot, the most useful exercise will be to experiment with hitting the cue ball against a rail, to see how it reacts. In time, try to estimate where you need to hit the ball against the rail for it to bounce off and disappear into the pocket. If the table has marks, this will clearly assist you as you attempt the shot.

If you play a natural shot to the rail, the cue ball will rebound off at the same, but opposite, angle of impact. If the rails are firm and in good condition, very little of the pace should be lost.

When players reach a certain level, they will be confident of potting a ball off more than one rail. If you see a professional practice their full repertoire of shots, they can play shots off three or four rails. But you should focus on playing shots off one rail for the time being.

Even those that play at a decent level might practice 15 or 20 bank shots in quick succession, hoping for at least a 75 percent success rate. If you are practicing with just the cue ball, and manage to pocket it with two attempts out of ten, this is a very fine start.

1887

Legendary billiards player Willie Hoppe is born. The American excelled at different forms of the game, including straight rail and three cushion.

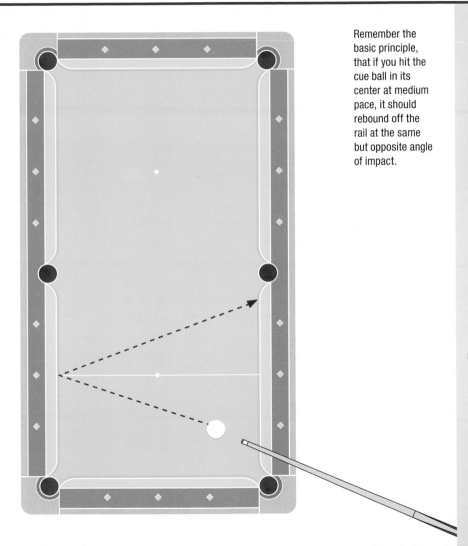

Remember the basic principle, that if you hit the cue ball in its center at medium pace, it should rebound off the rail at the same but opposite angle of impact.

A Level Playing Field?

Even at the very highest level, in any cue sport, players sometimes complain at a particular tournament that the rails are behaving oddly. They could either be too bouncy, with the balls flying off at pace, or too cushioned, with the balls losing their pace significantly when hitting the rail. This inconsistency is just one of the frustrations one might encounter when playing this game.

THE NAP

On most tables in the United States, the cloth consists of a nap-free fabric, and if this is the case, you won't need to worry. But on some cloths there is still a nap, or protruding weave, on the cloth, and it would be useful to determine the condition and direction of the nap before beginning to play.

You could place your hand flat on the table and move it down. You should find that the nap lays flat. When repeating the process, but moving your hand up the table, the nap should bristle up. The nap will not be so obvious on cloths that have been well used and have become worn.

When you hit a ball, the movement will cause friction as it moves over the cloth, which will increase when the cloth has a nap. When you play a shot with the nap, the pace of the cue ball will not be affected, but when you play against it a lightly paced ball may come to a stop more quickly.

Jordan Church

Control

You should try not to move the cue ball around too much, as you are inviting the opportunity for more things to go wrong—try to limit the movement of the cue ball. Always try to use the simplest option when playing a shot.

You should train your eyes to focus on the cue ball and object ball, fully aware of where you are aiming at all times. Don't let your concentration slip if possible, focusing all your attention on the balls and the table.

A Level Playing Field?

The Draw Shot

In simple terms, the direction that the cue ball takes after hitting the object ball can be dictated by where you strike the cue ball. The draw shot should be played when you want the cue ball to move backward after striking the object ball. In some places, you may hear people describing the draw shot as putting backspin on the ball. In other cue sports, such as snooker, it may be referred to as a screw shot.

If you are learning how to add draw, you are best off starting with natural, or straight, shots. You should place the cue ball around 15 inches away from the object ball, which you should put somewhere near a pocket. When the balls are closer together, it is generally easier to apply draw. As the balls are moved farther apart, you will see that the effect of draw is dramatically reduced.

When playing this type of shot, it is strongly advised to position your bridge hand slightly lower. Your fingertips should be moved farther apart, until your hand is virtually lying flat on the table. It is important to keep your cue parallel to the table.

When first playing this shot, it is likely that you will miscue it. This is natural as the process will seem strange. The likelihood is also that you will stab at the shot. Again the best advice will be to try and play the shot as smoothly as possible. There is a common misconception that for the shot to work out as desired, the cue ball will need to be struck with force. This is not necessarily the case—as is the case in most sports, and with most shots in pool, timing is the key.

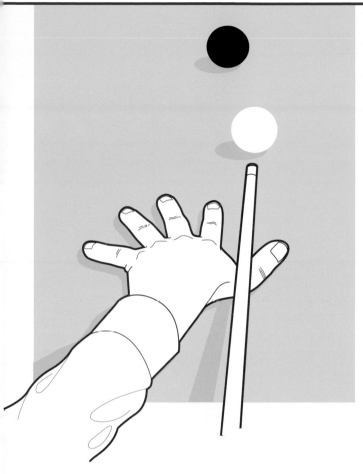

When playing the
draw shot, you
should be aiming
to hit the cue ball
below its center.
If the shot is hit
correctly, it should
have the effect
of making the
cue ball appear
to bounce back
from the object
ball. You will need
to play this shot
on a regular basis
during any game
of pool.

This is where your cue-chalking skills will come in handy. You should make sure your tip is covered with chalk, since this will assist greatly in your attempts to move the cue ball as desired. If a tip has no chalk on it, you will soon find that the cue ball won't move as far, if at all.

Another problem you may find at first is that you don't move the cue away quickly enough after playing the shot, and if you apply draw the cue ball will come back and hit it. In truth, you do have a fair amount of time to withdraw the cue, and this should just come with practice.

Broadly speaking, the reason that draw shots become easier when the cue ball is nearer to the object ball is that it gives less time for the spin to wear off. Think of it as giving the cue ball an instruction; on this occasion you have instructed it to move backward. Initially, the ball will move forward, even though the spin put on the ball means it is battling to pull back the other way. If the shot has been played right the cue ball will only react according to instruction when it has made contact with the object ball.

The draw shot is much easier to play when the balls are straight, and you are not trying to pot an object ball at an angle. You will have to apply more draw to the ball when the ball is at a slight angle, when you are hitting the ball with half-face contact, for example. When the balls are at a very extreme angle, the cue ball has too much work to do as it is, and any draw put on the shot will have little effect.

Shot Technique

You should try not to hit the cue ball too low when applying draw, as this could easily spoil your shot (by scooping underneath the ball and causing it to jump). You should cue straight, making sure you don't jab at the ball. The cue should travel past the cue ball by 2 to 3 inches. Timing is key to the success of this shot, and your action should remain smooth.

Keep focused and take your time with each shot.

The Draw Shot

Putting English on the Ball

Another important skill to learn when playing pool is the ability to put 'English' on the ball. This is known as sidespin, or simply side, in some parts of the world. To apply English, you need to strike the cue ball to the left or right of center, depending on which way you want it to move. When English is applied properly, it can have a number of important effects.

The cue ball can slightly change direction before it makes contact with the object ball. When players become highly proficient at using English, they sometimes apply it when the object ball is slightly blocked behind another ball, putting enough on to allow the cue ball to squeeze past and reach its target.

But if you are starting out, it is best to try something easier than that. As well as the cue ball changing path before it hits an object ball, it can do so after making contact with an object ball, particularly when bouncing off a rail. This can be an extremely useful skill to learn when you are looking to pot a ball and gain good position for your following shot. One of the best ways to start practicing is to hit the cue ball toward a rail with English. If you hit the cue ball on the right-hand side, it will deflect to the right off the rail.

1908

Cowboy pool—a game played with just four balls, a hybrid of English billiards and pool —is first mentioned in a rule book.

The contact between cue ball and object ball is also affected when playing the ball with English. If you apply right-hand English, the object ball will deviate slightly to the left. If the shot is played properly, it still shouldn't mean a pot is missed.

Using English correctly can be extremely useful if you find yourself snookered during a game, when your intended object ball is hidden by one or more of your opponent's balls. Playing the cue ball with English can enable it to deflect to one side or the other off a rail and reach your intended target.

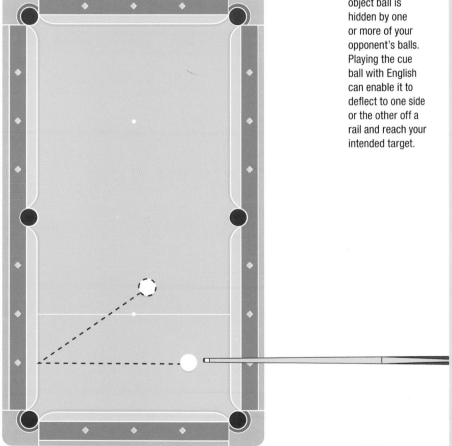

Applying English to the ball can be a difficult skill to master, and it is imperative that a beginner makes sure they are first comfortable with the other basics of the game.

Even when you want the cue ball to deviate significantly, it isn't necessary to hit it on its extreme edge. A useful exercise at first might be to play across the table and

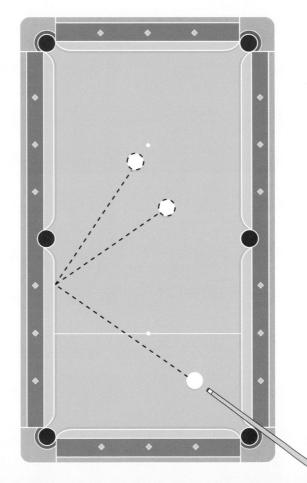

apply enough English for the cue ball to deflect to the right and land in the center pocket.

You can also try to play the cue ball with right-hand English at an angle to the rail, giving you a better idea of how the angle of rebound can be increased. You can use a particular part of the table as a marker for aiming, like the foot spot or a corner pocket.

It is important that you practice applying English on both sides, so if you have begun with hitting the right-hand side of the cue ball, hit the left of it also, to apply English the other way. When you start to get used to this, the chances are you will gain some satisfaction from the ball taking a particular course off the rail. Again you may want to

try to apply left-hand English with an angled shot to the rail.

The reasons for controlling the ball in a game of pool are plain to see, and in simple terms it is all about making the maximum use of your innings at the table. When you are feeling more confident, you may want to experiment with two object balls on the table, applying draw or English to pot one ball and trying to set yourself up for another.

You might even want to combine the draw and English shots in one shot which, if played properly, will have the effect of spinning the ball backward from the object ball and deflecting off a rail in a particular direction.

The temptation will be to hit the ball toward its extreme edges and either miss it completely or miscue. This would be understandable, but it should be remembered that it isn't necessary. If you want the cue ball to move slightly to the right after contacting a rail, you only need to hit it very slightly to the right of center.

Applying Topspin

Sometimes you will want to follow through with the cue ball, in other words for the cue ball to continue on its same path after making contact with the object ball. To do this you should be aiming for the top of the cue ball, applying topspin to it. Again the temptation might be to aim for the extreme top of the cue ball, but this isn't necessary. Aiming just above center would normally be sufficient for the shot you are attempting.

The bridge hand should be slightly raised for this shot, with fingertips moved closer together and the middle of your hand lifted. The cue should remain in its ideal position, parallel to the table. This shot will be most effective when the balls are lined up straight with a pocket. When there is more angle, the spin put on the ball will have less effect.

Once again, the successful shot will not necessarily be about pace, but timing and accuracy. In many situations, gentle follow-through can leave you nicely lined up for your following shot. When the cue ball and object balls are close to each other, you would be looking to strike the cue ball just slightly above center. When the balls are farther apart, you need to work harder to achieve your aims and will need to strike the cue ball at a higher point.

Many times during an average game you won't want or need to move the cue ball in any given direction, but will aim for it to stay still after

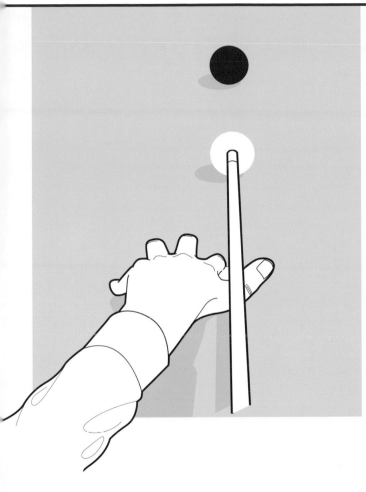

You should be careful when faced with a straight shot and applying topspin, as the cue ball will follow the object ball into the pocket if the shot is played too hard or you aim too high on the cue ball. You would then have committed a foul, and given your opponent an advantage, which could have been easily avoided.

contacting the object ball. This is referred to as a stun shot, and should work out nicely if you aim for the center of the ball. If the cue ball and object balls are farther apart, you should aim very slightly below the center of the ball, applying the smallest amount of draw to the shot.

More Advanced Shots

It will take you some time to get used to applying draw, English, and topspin to the ball. When you are feeling comfortable, there are some more difficult shots that you might want to try. You won't play these shots as regularly during a game, but it will certainly be good to have them as part of your repertoire.

THE SWERVE SHOT

The aim of the swerve shot is to curve the line of play of the cue ball. This shot is played by selecting a target spot at the base of the ball, either left or right of its center, and playing a stab shot with some force.

You should first adopt your normal stance, then raise your cue out of parallel to the table, at an angle of about 45 degrees from the bed of the table. You can do this by bending your right foot until your weight is taken on the ball of that foot. The bridge hand should be raised more significantly for this shot, with the fingers in a more upright position and just touching the cloth. As you swing the cue back, you may feel your shoulder muscles tighten.

The tendency at this point is often to allow your arm to swing out, but you should keep your arm tight to your body. As the target spot is low and off-center it is vital that your aim is steady.

As you swing back, you will feel your balance pushed forward into your bridge hand. Your stance can move out of balance if you delay the shot too long.

You then need to play a stab shot, with the action stopping the instant the cue strikes the ball. You can help control the forward swing by tightening your grip. You can try practicing this shot by placing a ball in between the cue ball and the object ball. You should note that it is extremely difficult indeed to control the cue ball or object ball after impact. The idea of the shot is generally to escape trouble that you may find yourself in during a game.

You should place the cue ball in the head area and your intended object ball toward the other end of the table. Place the black 8-ball in between these two balls, so the object ball cannot be hit directly without needing to swerve the cue ball. Practice the swerve shot, trying to bend the cue ball around the 8-ball and hitting the object ball a number of times. You should try not to become frustrated if you fail to execute the shot properly at first, because it certainly takes some time to master this shot.

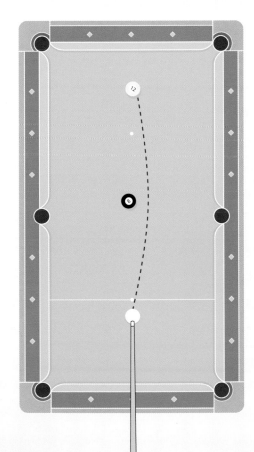

JUMPING THE CUE BALL

Sometimes you may need to jump the cue ball in order to reach an object ball. This is a shot that requires very careful and accurate cueing. The best way to play this shot is to hit the cue ball down onto the bed of the table with sufficient power for it to bounce back up and over a ball or balls that might be blocking your intended target.

Your bridge hand should be raised, and the cue elevated. The angle to which the cue will be raised will depend on how quickly you need to jump the ball. If a ball blocking your path is close to the cue ball, you will want the cue ball to begin lifting immediately. Because of the power needed to force the cue

ball over another ball and reach its target, you will need to play this shot firmly.

The jabbing, or stabbing, action used for this shot will also come in handy when you find yourself needing to bridge over another ball to strike the cue ball.

This shot is fraught with difficulty, since you need to form a high bridge, with your fingers as close to the offending object ball as possible. To gain height for this shot, you should raise your stance by bending your right foot (if a right-handed player) and take a small part of your weight on the ball of your foot. Most of your weight will be far forward and taken on the extended fingers of your bridge hand. The cue needs to be held at around 45 degrees to the table. You need to make a stab shot at the cue ball, targeting a spot just below the center of the ball.

1913

An American silent film, *A Game of Pool*, starring Edgar Kennedy and Fred Mace, is believed to be the first film ever made about the sport.

USING A MECHANICAL BRIDGE

Another part of the game you will want to practice is to play the shot with the aid of a mechanical bridge, or a rest as it is sometimes called, particularly in Britain. In truth, this looks more difficult than it is, with the rest forming a perfect "V" and giving you the chance to focus on your grip and lining up the shot.

Handling a mechanical bridge does, however, require some thought and care. If you aren't careful when placing it on the table, or when removing it after a shot has been played, the danger is that you may hit another ball with it and commit a foul.

An old-fashioned term used to describe the awkward position of having the cue ball blocked by another ball directly behind it is to say that a player is "Chinese snookered."

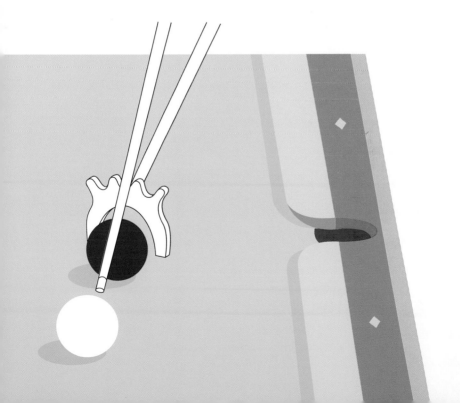

The Masse Shot

The masse shot will almost certainly take a long time to play properly. Similar to a swerve shot, this will be played when the only route to your object ball is to send your cue ball traveling 180 degrees in a tight circle around another ball that is blocking its path. You would play the shot in a similar fashion to the swerve shot, but with the cue held at an upright angle, adding a large amount of spin.

You should stand close to the table, and if you are a right-handed player you should move your right leg back and bend the foot, keeping the left leg straight to take your weight.

The bridging is just as awkward for this shot. You should lean slightly forward over the table, keeping your bridging arm straight. You should face the palm of your hand away from the table and extend your fingers, and form a triangular support with three fingers. You should use your little finger to add support to the bridge. You will not be able to easily form the "V" with your thumb, so the cue must be guided down the joint of the first finger and thumb.

You will target a spot near the top of the cue ball. Grip your cue tightly and raise the cue almost upright to the table. If the grip is too uncomfortable, use a lower position. When you make the backswing your arm will tend to move out, so control this as much as you can. Rotating your wrist can sometimes help.

Your downward swing will be a stabbing action and it must be powerful enough to give the cue ball the extreme spin it needs for the shot. The

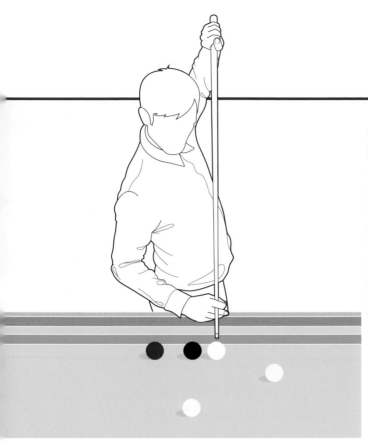

A good way to practice can be to place a layer or two of cardboard over the table until you can fully control the downward cueing action. This should prevent any possible damage to the cloth and cue tip.

ball will move slightly forward on impact and, as the spin takes over, it will move in a tight circle due to the effect of the spin. The most you can expect from this extremely difficult defensive shot is to hit your object ball—to gain position from it would be to expect too much.

It is right and proper that the description of this shot falls at the end of the chapter, because you should only be attempting the masse when you are fully confident of the more basic shots that you will need to use, like the draw and English. If you are playing the masse with any degree of success, it will undoubtedly give you great confidence and suggests that you could well be a big hit on the pool table.

Chapter Four: ADVANCED PLAY

Your practice is going well, and you have a good idea of the basics. But how will you approach playing the game? What are the more advanced shots you need to play? How important is the safety game? And what about the all-important mental side of pool?

Once you are satisfied that you have mastered the basic skills, it is time to consider stepping your game up a gear and learning to take advantage of different states of play.

The Break

When you are happy with the various skills you now have at your disposal, you can think about beginning to use them in real situations, during a game of pool. There will come a time when you will only learn how to play certain shots while playing a game, rather than in practice.

The initial shot, the break, can set the tone for any game. If you watch top players in action, you will see that a successful break can be sufficient to win them the game. For most of us, we are just hoping for a positive start to the game. It should be said that while the toss of a coin can sometimes determine who breaks, you may on occasion need to "win the lag." This should certainly be the case if you are taking part in any form of competition. This involves hitting the cue

ball from the kitchen area, or baulk line, toward the foot rail and back toward the head rail. The player who hits the cue ball closest to the head rail breaks first. The lag can provide the perfect early test of how well you are cueing.

The days of a more negative break shot, where you would try and leave the cue ball in a safe position or avoid splitting the balls too much, now tend to belong to the past. This is largely because the rules require a certain number of balls to hit the rails, or a certain number to cross the center line and into the bottom half of the table. The rules now state that at least four balls must connect with a rail if no ball is pocketed.

The desired result of a break shot is to pot at least one ball. I'm sure that many of you reading this have played in eight-ball games where your opponent has claimed victory when you have potted the black 8-ball off the break shot. The rules state that in this case, the shooter has the option of spotting the 8-ball or re-racking the balls. In nine-ball pool, you actually win the game if the 9-ball is potted off a break shot.

Players will experiment with different positions, but the preferred method is still to place the cue ball on or near the head spot, and aim for the ball at the front of the rack. You should aim to hit the ball full in the face, or just slightly off full. If a ball flies into a pocket, you should always consider it a bonus. You have early control of the table. In eight-ball pool, the table is still "open" and you would have the choice of whether to pot a stripe or a solid with your next shot.

Broadly speaking, the break shot remains something of a lottery. Generally, it is worth approaching the break in a positive fashion. Some players prefer a soft break, which still leaves some of the balls in a cluster and pushes the cue ball back toward the head rail. But this shot can easily go wrong, particularly if a player is inexperienced, by not pushing enough balls toward the rails.

Selecting Shots

Shot selection is absolutely key in any game of pool. If you want to improve in this area, the best way is simply to gain experience. If you are playing eight-ball, there will often be more than one ball available to pot, and it won't always be desirable to select the easier option first. You should always try to remember that the only prizes handed out are when you pot the final ball. Each ball potted before that is simply a small step taken toward the crucial conclusion to any game, and you should always approach each shot with overall victory in mind.

If you are playing eight-ball, it will sometimes be sensible to leave

a relatively simple pot for a subsequent visit to the table, particularly if a ball lies near a pocket. You might want to consider developing one of your more awkwardly placed balls, moving it into a position where it will be easier to pot later on in the game.

You might on occasion consider attempting to pot the most difficult ball of all. If one lies against a rail, for example, you might want to push it toward the pocket. It will either

Gospel according to...
Jordan Church

Closed Bridge

The closed bridge can be useful when you are playing a shot with the cue ball stuck against a cushion. Grip the cushion as if you are simply grabbing it, tucking your thumb under the hand. The cue can be placed between the index finger and middle finger, giving you as much control as possible. Keep the cue parallel to the table if possible, and try not to dig down on the ball.

drop in, giving you the best possible outcome, or finish up somewhere near or over the pocket. This will set the ball up nicely for you later in the game, particularly if you are left with no other decent chance to pot a ball in a future inning.

You should also keep a keen eye on your opponent's balls as well. It won't do you any

good in the long term to pot one of your own balls, but by doing so deflect toward one of theirs and push it into a convenient position. You should never be afraid to use your new skills to help you, applying draw or English where necessary to move the cue ball to where you would like it to be after potting a ball.

It will always be sensible to simply take a step back and take stock of the situation. You can walk around the table and look at all the balls. Try to gauge how many of your balls are in positions from which they can be potted.

Selecting Shots

The Plant

Sometimes a pot won't be readily available, and you may need to manufacture a shot in order to pocket a ball. A plant (or "combination shot") involves playing one object ball onto another one to pocket it.

In nine-ball pool you are allowed to pot any ball on the table at any time, providing you first make contact with the lowest numbered ball available. Sometimes the balls might line up perfectly to make the plant—they might even be touching each other. The skill is to identify these balls—sometimes they can be missed, especially if they are surrounded by a cluster of other balls. This goes to show again how important it can be to take a step back and size up the situation.

The balls will sometimes need to be made into a plant, because they are an inch or two away from each other. This requires more accuracy with cueing. If the balls are lined up with a pocket, the shot will be easier, but you will on occasion need to hit the second ball at an angle.

The principle behind a plant is pretty simple: you will want the first ball to connect with the second ball at exactly the same angle as you would have needed to hit that ball with the cue ball were you aiming for a normal pot. The shot becomes harder when the balls are farther apart, and if they are any more than 4 or 5 inches apart the chances of missing

1941

Willie Mosconi, arguably the sport's most legendary name and a man credited with helping to bring it to the masses, wins his first World Straight Pool Championship.

are high. This is especially true if the angle needs to be changed considerably.

You might want to try lining up balls to practice the plant. Here you should aim for the first red ball, playing a natural shot, with medium pace and a slight amount of draw. The first ball should hit the second red ball and drive it into the pocket.

In a game of nine-ball pool, you could claim victory at any time with a carefully played plant shot, if you hit the lowest numbered ball on the table and use it to hit the 9-ball into the pocket.

Putting it All Together

The next exercise will test a number of your skills. You should set the balls up as shown in the illustration. You should play a shot with moderate pace to strike the 11-ball slightly off full-face, so that it connects with the 8-ball and pockets it. Ideally the cue ball will then continue to the foot rail, and rebound to just below the foot spot.

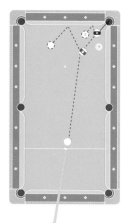

The 11-ball should now be played with medium pace and some slight left-hand English, hitting the ball at three-quarter face. The cue ball should bounce off the foot rail and then return to around 3 or 4 inches above the foot spot. The 6-ball should then be pocketed, using medium pace and some slight right-hand English, leaving the cue ball

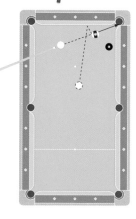

to return to mid-table after bouncing off the foot rail.

A successful plant will pocket the second ball after contact with the first, but sometimes the first ball can be pocketed by successfully deflecting off another. This will often be the case when a ball is near a pocket. You can practice placing one ball near a pocket and hitting the first ball at the right angle for it to deflect off that ball and fly into the pocket.

While at first you should concentrate simply on making sure a ball disappears into a pocket, you should in time also think about your position for the following shot. It is always important to think ahead; to your next shot, and to the general situation in any game you are playing.

It can be easy on occasion to let yourself drift through a game, particularly if it seems that you have an advantage. But complacency in the game of pool can be fatal, because your opponent can quickly seize the initiative.

You may not succeed with this exercise straight away, but in time you should be executing the shots correctly. It will give you a good idea of the need to play not just one good shot, but sometimes two or three in succession, to win a game of pool.

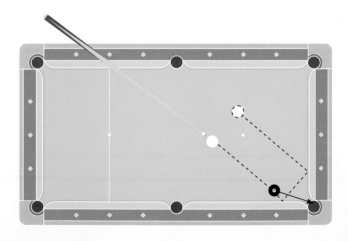

Using Bank Shots

The practice shots that you played earlier while learning the basics will be extremely useful when you are faced with a real game situation. You will soon find that you need to regularly play bank shots, and playing them well will be a valuable weapon in your armory. Many players, particularly those who play the game at a fun level, still see a successful bank shot as a fluke. This would be a mistake on their part, since a properly played shot requires careful planning and execution.

A bank shot is still one that carries with it a degree of risk; mainly because you are putting some faith in how the ball bounces off a rail,

and this is not always within your total control. But if the shot is played with deliberate and calculated care, you are giving yourself the best possible chance of achieving the desired outcome.

To practice, place the cue ball in the head area of the table, and the object ball on the head string. Don't try to hit the ball too hard, as this will not help the object ball into the pocket. Timing and accuracy are key to these shots. Aim for the center of the object ball and become as familiar as you can with the angles and how the balls bounce off the rail.

Try this shot 20 times in succession—if you are successful with ten or more attempts this is highly impressive. You will see in time that careful and accurate cueing, and not luck, will help the object ball into the

1950

The pool world is in mourning as one of the sport's great early stars, Ralph Greenleaf, dies at the age of 50.

pocket. You might even find that you are enjoying playing bank shots so much that you start to attempt them from all angles. Be careful though, as missing one can often leave your opponent with an easy pot and control of the table. You should only play a bank shot when necessary, when the direct line to the object ball is obscured. Any skilled player will prefer to play more natural shots, but will know that a successful bank shot can sometimes open up a game sufficiently for them to go on and claim victory.

You could try more difficult bank shots when you are feeling more comfortable with the process. Place an object ball near a center pocket and use your knowledge of angles to judge where to hit the cue ball against a rail for it to bounce off and carom the ball into the pocket. It would be helpful to stand between the two balls before playing the shot, looking at the opposite rail and trying to judge the angle.

It clearly won't always be the case that bank shots

line up nicely for you, and sometimes a shot has to be manufactured, or made. You should also try to pot an object ball with a bank shot by hitting it with three-quarter face contact. Try setting the balls up again, but moving the cue ball around 6 inches down the table away from the head spot. The angle won't be natural this time, and you will have to do more work with the cue ball.

You could also practice playing a shot with English, altering the direction that

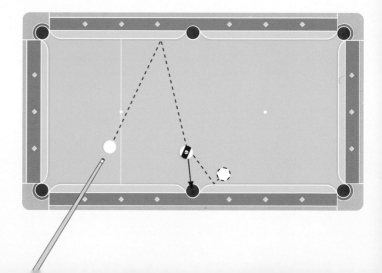

the cue ball will take after bouncing off the rail. You should place an object ball over a center pocket and experiment with how much English you need to apply to the cue ball for it to bounce off the rail and pot that ball.

It is more common during a game that you will play a bank shot to one of the center pockets, but it certainly won't do you any harm to try playing one of these shots into a corner pocket. As you gain experience, you will realize that shots can bounce off the rails and disappear into a pocket using all kinds of angles.

Playing a shot off five rails will look impossible at first, and it certainly isn't recommended that you practice this shot much until you are at a decent level. In time, however, you will see that if played correctly it is possible for the cue ball to bounce off five rails and hit an object ball that has been placed over a pocket.

In years gone by, players referred to a shot played off five rails as a "five bank cocked hat."

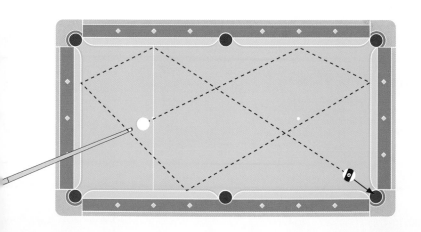

Snookered!

There will be times when you will need to use the rail not only to pot a ball, but to escape from a snooker. When you are snookered it means that you will be unable to make contact with your intended object ball because it is blocked by another ball. You can find yourself snookered, or hooked, at any time during a game. This can be the result of a fortunate accident on the part of your opponent. It could be, however, that your opponent has deliberately left you snookered because they didn't have a decent chance to pot any ball.

When you find yourself snookered, it can sometimes come as a shock, particularly if you seemed to be in control of the game, but a well-played kick shot can get you out of trouble, no matter how difficult the situation might seem.

Again, the simple principle applies, namely that the angle at which a ball strikes the rail is the same as the angle at which it leaves the rail. This is again presuming that the cue ball has been hit naturally, in its center. If any spin has been applied to the ball, it will behave differently when bouncing off the rail.

The pace at which you strike the cue ball can also slightly change the direction that the cue ball will take after bouncing off a rail. When the ball has been played with more pace than is usually the case, the cue ball can straighten after impact with a rail.

1959

Jean Balukas, one of the greatest women players of all time, is born in Brooklyn, New York. She played the game from an extremely young age, and was already wowing crowds when she was just six years old.

It should normally be possible to escape when you are snookered by judging the angles, and hitting the cue ball naturally to kick off a rail. But there are times when you will need to put English on the ball, because another ball is blocking a straighter path to the object ball. You will sometimes need to use more than one rail to escape from a snooker, and this will require you to judge the angles perfectly. You should always remember that the same principles will apply: a ball will bounce off a rail at the same angle at which it hit it.

Leaving snookers for your opponent on purpose can require real skill and accuracy, particularly since the rules don't allow you to just roll the cue ball up behind another. You have to make sure either the cue ball or an object ball hits a rail for any shot where no ball is pocketed.

More Work With the Rails

You may sometimes see more skilled players hitting the ball to within a few inches of a pocket and hitting rails on either side of it, to bounce out of the jaws. This is a highly risky shot, and requires real skill. You could practice this clever shot by hitting the cue ball toward a pocket, but purposely missing it and judging how the balls react when bouncing off both rails.

As well as being snookered behind a ball or balls, you may also be "corner hooked," with the cue ball trapped in the jaws of a pocket, and one of the jaws blocking your path to the intended object ball. Again, you can escape trouble with a well-played kick shot, bearing in mind that you will need to be extra careful playing the shot because cueing will be difficult with the cue ball in such an awkward position.

POTTING BALLS

During an average game, some balls will inevitably stick to the rails. Potting a ball along a rail tends to require more skill and accuracy than potting one that is in a more open position on the table, but it isn't a shot that you should approach with fear.

Most pockets these days are pretty generous, particularly on the bigger tables, and give you every chance of potting a ball. When faced with a ball that is stuck to a rail, you need to make doubly sure of hitting the object ball in the right place. If the cue ball is also stuck against a rail, it won't move away from the rail after connecting with the object ball because the shot is straight. You shouldn't worry about that, and instead focus on making the pot.

The temptation is to hit the cue ball hard when faced with trying to pot a ball along the rail, but the chances are that this won't help your cause. A cue ball hit with slow to medium pace will give the object ball more chance of dropping into the pocket. Hitting the ball more gently will generally give you more control over the accuracy of the shot.

If you face having to try to pot a ball with the cue ball tight against a rail, remember to keep your bridge hand in the same position, but with the thumb moved behind the rail if it isn't big enough to feel comfortable, or your bridge hand raised with fingers in an upright position if that feels more natural.

It is still possible to make decent contact from this position, but you won't be able to put any control on the cue ball. Instead you should focus all your attention on making good contact with the intended object ball.

If the cue ball is away from the rail and the object ball stuck to it, you should hit the object ball at an angle; you will often need to hit it with a quarter-face contact. If this is the case, the cue ball should bounce away from the rail, making the next shot easier.

Thinking Ahead

An enjoyable way to practice can be to place five or six balls on the table and use your skills to try to negotiate your way around the table. The good player will always be thinking about the position for their next shot. In a game situation, you will often find yourself struggling early on, with your opponent potting most of the balls.

This won't necessarily mean that you will lose the game, however. You could still be left with a good chance to clear the table to win later in the game. You should always keep in mind that potting the final ball will be key, and in nine-ball pool you are only ever potentially one shot away from victory.

Try placing four balls close to each other, all close to one corner pocket.

While you may find yourself focusing totally on potting the balls at first, you will soon want to consider position for the next ball in the set. You could use draw for the purpose, or judge the angles

Working Back

If you are working out a clearance, the best advice is often to work backward, beginning with the shot you intend to leave yourself with on the final ball, and ending with the shot you are facing first.

Sometimes, particularly when starting out in the game, it can be tempting to simply pot everything on offer. It is often sensible, however, to play the long game, to refuse a simple shot, for example, if you know that the next shot is fraught with danger.

and bounce the cue ball off a rail or two. You should continue with this exercise until you have potted all four balls in succession—it will certainly be a good test of your patience as well as your pool skills.

On occasion it will be necessary to take on a difficult pot. This will generally be when you feel that any miss will be pounced on by your opponent, since most of the balls are generously placed on the table. You may feel that a pot is the only option, because there is no way of playing a decent safety shot. You might need to pot your way out of trouble, knowing that if you managed to pot a difficult ball it could open up a big chance to go on and clear the remaining balls to win the game.

Thinking Ahead

Breaking Up a Cluster

Sometimes the balls will all seem to be in awkward positions on the table, but one or two carefully played positional shots can quickly turn them back in your favor.

You may find that three or four balls are tucked up together in a cluster, but you could think about disturbing these after potting a ball.

You should carefully weigh up the angles, and see if there is a natural way you can pot a ball and get the cue ball to bounce off a rail and into the cluster. It may be that the angle is not natural, and you will have to manufacture it slightly using cue-ball control.

A small amount of English applied to the cue ball

could make all the difference.

When your intention is to disturb a cluster of balls, you should consider the shot carefully. If there are a number of balls in the cluster, a shot played with power could well be more beneficial as there needs to be enough pace on the cue ball to sufficiently disturb the cluster of balls.

If there are fewer balls in the cluster, it can often be more effective to use slow pace and be able to predict with more accuracy where the balls will be heading after contact.

After finding yourself in an awkward position, one carefully played shot can open up the game and even give you the chance of going on to clear the table. It should be your intention

Cluster shots will always contain an element of luck, no matter how carefully you plan the shot or how accurate your cueing is. You just have to give yourself the best possible chance of splitting up the awkward balls. You could find that if the shot works out, three or four balls have suddenly been moved into more open positions from which they can be potted.

never to waste a shot. If you see the chance to develop your position after potting a ball, you should try to use it.

Once you begin to master the various ways that the cue ball can be controlled, you should always be looking to use those skills to help your position on the table.

Positioning

While nobody should fear potting a ball down the rail, it could make life easier if you move one away from the rail into a more open position. Again, the angle can sometimes allow you to pot a ball naturally and then deflect toward another, pushing it into the middle of the table. It would be sensible to assess the overall situation before playing such a shot. If it is easy enough to pot a ball and position the cue ball behind the next ball on a rail, it might not be worth trying to push a ball away from a rail.

If, for example, you are playing a game of nine-ball and are aiming to pot the 4-ball, while getting in a good position to pot the 5-ball, it would be worth checking where the other balls are on the table. If the 6-ball is over a pocket, it might not be worth taking too great a risk, as you might be leaving your opponent with two easy

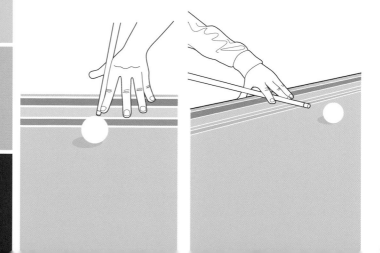

shots if you miss with your attempt to pot the 5-ball.

If you are aiming to pot the 4-ball, the 5-ball is over the pocket, and the 6-ball is in an awkward position, it might well be worth trying to disturb the 6-ball while potting the 4-ball. If the shot goes wrong, and you don't manage to make decent contact with the 6-ball, you have the security of knowing that the 5-ball is over the pocket. You should not only have a relatively simple chance to knock the 5-ball in, but will still have a good chance to come off at an angle to set yourself up for the 6-ball.

Always be aware of where the 9-ball is on the table. If possible, you want to avoid being in the situation of having potted five or six balls but leaving yourself with a difficult shot on the 9-ball. You face the prospect of missing, leaving your opponent to pinch the game despite having dones most of the hard work during the game. You should look for ways to develop an awkwardly positioned 9-ball if at all possible.

Safety Play

It should be remembered that, first and foremost, pool is an attacking game. All you have to do is watch the professionals at work and you will see that at the top level of the game attacking play is the dominant feature. One, or maybe two, visits to the table are sometimes all that is required to win a game. But in time you will notice that there are many games that are also characterized by safety play, particularly at the start.

At the more fun level, games of pool tend to last that little while longer, but the majority of players will still be looking to pot balls first, and establish a winning position on the table with attacking play.

1961

The film *The Hustler* is shown in cinemas across America, and leads to a huge surge of interest in the game. Pool halls throughout the nation are packed out this year.

Despite the fact that new rules are often brought in to encourage a more attacking approach, one should never dismiss safety play, a part of the game that can sometimes be overlooked. Most of us would like to be as offensive as possible at all times, but the situation in a particular game doesn't always lend itself to an attacking shot. You can play safe from the start in nine-ball pool, by playing the special "push-out" shot (see page 214) immediately after the break. You don't have to make contact with another ball, or a rail, with this shot.

If you are left with a difficult shot on your chosen object ball at any stage of the game, you might be wise to think about playing safe. Perhaps you are faced with needing a bank shot at a tough angle, or a very fine cut. It might not always be worth the risk to attempt a pot, because if you miss, it could leave the table at the mercy of your opponent.

A well-executed safety shot, on the other hand, can put your opponent in trouble, and force them to make a mistake with their next shot. The table could then be left open for you to take control of the game, or maybe even win it. So in essence, when you are playing safe, you should be thinking that if you get the shot right, there is the genuine prospect that you will reap the rewards of a good shot in your next inning.

Many of the game's newer rules have forced a more attacking approach to be taken. You may still see some players of more mature vintage adopting a negative approach to the game—rolling up behind one of their balls to leave their opponent snookered for example. But they will often also play with other outdated rules.

DEALING WITH A CLUSTER

You may find during a game that your next object ball is tucked up in a cluster of balls, making it impossible to pot it. You could consider an aggressive safety shot, splitting the balls up to push them all into more open positions.

However, a safety shot won't necessarily be poor or disappointing if you leave your opponent with a difficult chance to pot their next ball. If you leave your opponent with a risky pot, there remains a very good chance that they will miss and leave the ball open for you to attempt a pot.

If you are playing nine-ball pool, and there is no chance of potting your next object ball, the best option might be to push it toward a cluster of other balls, making sure your opponent can't pot it. The chances are that your opponent will be forced to split that cluster open with their next shot, and if it isn't judged properly they could again leave you with a good chance in your next inning.

AN EYE ON THE FINAL BALL

Depending on the situation in the game, you might want to consider where the final ball is situated. If you seem to be in a losing position, or on the back foot in a game of eight-ball pool, it might well be in your interest to keep that final ball in an awkward position on the table. On the other hand, you may feel the game is pretty even, or that you are slightly in the ascendancy. You might then want to try to bring the final ball into a more open position, presuming that you will be first to have an attempt at potting it. You can develop that ball while potting another ball, greatly increasing your chance of winning that game during your current inning.

An element of good safety play is weighing up the risks, which involves tempting your opponent into taking on a difficult chance on occasion. Any player will be well aware of the pressure if they know a missed pot is likely to leave their opponent with a good chance.

Making Life Hard for Your Opponent

Ideally you will want to play a safety shot that leaves your opponent with a very tricky shot to play next. Leaving your opponent snookered will not always be possible, but there are other ways to make their shot awkward. This is where those first practices at hitting the cue ball will come in handy, since you may need to time the safety shot well to leave your opponent in trouble.

As well as leaving balls tucked together in a cluster, you could make trouble for your opponent by leaving the cue ball or object ball, preferably both, near a rail. You should also try to ensure, if possible, that there is considerable distance between the cue ball and the object ball, since any shot is more difficult to control when this is the case.

LAYING SNOOKERS

Laying snookers is not something that comes easily, particularly for those players that haven't got a great amount of experience, but if there are a number of balls on the table you do have more likelihood of pulling this off. The exercise featured opposite, taken from a game of nine-ball, shows a good example of playing the percentages, or "the long game," and leaving your opponent snookered.

There is a simple shot available on the 3-ball, but position on the 4-ball is going to be extremely difficult to obtain because it is being blocked by so many other balls. You should consider hitting the 3-ball with quarter-face impact, and a small amount of left-hand English. You have then snookered your opponent, and whatever happens afterward you should be left with the advantage.

Your opponent could easily miss with their attempt to escape the snooker, leaving you with ball in hand (see page 134). They could escape the snooker and hit the 3-ball, but even if they do there is a good chance it will bounce away from the rail and over the center pocket, leaving you with a chance to pot it, disturb some other balls, and give yourself a chance of potting the 4-ball.

Careful planning and foresight can often engineer a winning position. There will never be anything wrong with approaching a shot with a view to making your opponent's life as awkward as possible.

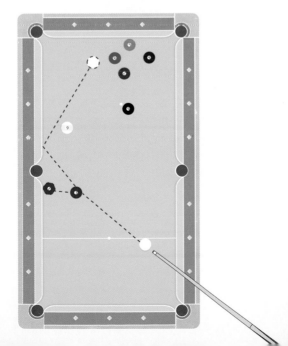

The Benefits of Playing Safe

Some players can become obviously frustrated if a game is becoming too negative, or even if you have the temerity to play a tactical shot, with the emphasis on safety. This is something that you should try your best to ignore. Good safety play and careful forward thinking should always be part of the repertoire of somebody serious about succeeding at the game of pool.

We can all miss the obvious at times during a game, and sometimes because we only have eyes for the next pot. This can sometimes be a ball that is easy to pot, and we are all too anxious to get straight down and knock it in—as if it will somehow disappear off the table if we don't. As you gain more experience, you will realize that it is just as important to focus on maintaining a good position for your next shot, or any situation you might be faced with a couple of shots down the line.

You should keep in mind the prospect not only of potting a ball but, if the angle is appropriate, bringing another ball out into the open at the same time. You might not be able to pot the ball you brought out into the open immediately, but the chances are that you might later in the game. No visit to the table should be wasted, because on every occasion you can improve your chances of eventually emerging as the winner.

If you play a reckless shot, it will only offer encouragement to your opponent. It could also mean that you are becoming frustrated, or rattled, with the state of the game. You should remember that many times on a pool table you can retrieve a negative situation with careful thought and planning.

You should weigh up each situation on its merits, and consider carefully which shot to play next. Have a look at the table below, taken from a game of blackball. Which shot would you play? You could consider hitting the red ball into the center pocket and using draw to bring the cue ball back for the red ball on the side rail. After potting the red along the side rail, you could aim for the red on the foot rail, either attempting a difficult pot or, more sensibly, leaving the cue ball tight against the rail and making it difficult for your opponent to pot a ball with their next shot.

Good safety exchanges, more than anything, show that pool is very much a game that is played in the head as well as on the table. Always cast your eyes across the whole table and watch every ball on it. If necessary, walk around the table and have a look at it from different angles.

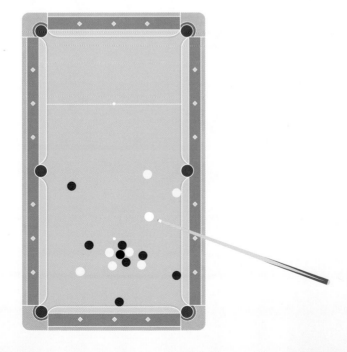

The Benefits of Playing Safe

Reading the Game

The game of pool can sometimes be deceptive, particularly to the untrained eye. A particular game can turn in an instant, and you should beware of developing a false sense of security about seeming to be in control of the table.

It should be remembered that in nine-ball a player can pot the 9-ball to win at any time, as long as they first hit the designated object ball (which will be the lowest number on the table at any given time). This gives the game an interesting dimension, particularly if the 9-ball happens to land over a pocket off the break, or early in the game. Players will often be looking for angles or paths toward the 9-ball from that moment onward.

There is not always gain in the long run by successfully potting the 4-, 5-, and 6-balls, if the 7-ball is blocked by another ball or is tight against a rail. A poor shot on the 7-ball could leave your opponent with just three balls needed to win the game. You should always be looking ahead and seeing how you could win the game, in subsequent innings at the table if not your current one.

In eight-ball, a player might appear to be on red-hot form, potting four or five of their balls before their opponent has potted any. But that may be no good to them in the long run if their remaining balls are in difficult situations. They

1976

The US Open Nine-Ball Championship is held for the first time in this year. The event is won by the brilliant American star Mike Sigel.

may have just been clearing a path for their opponent's balls to be potted.

If your opponent commits a foul you could be left with ball in hand, and a number of your balls might be in decent positions. In blackball you could be left with two shots if your opponent has fouled. You could take what is effectively a free shot if you wanted, particularly if one of your balls is awkwardly placed, and you will often win with one inning.

The experienced player will know that they sometimes need to bide their time, and that it is not necessarily a disadvantage to be left with the majority of balls on the table. There may be more chance to leave your opponent in trouble, possibly even snookered.

When Not to Pot

A time-honored tradition in eight-ball pool is to intentionally leave your balls over the pockets, making it impossible for your opponent to pass them with one of their balls. Sometimes it can be more beneficial to leave a ball on the pocket instead of potting it. This could potentially help you to clear the table in one inning. This can sometimes be a negative, but necessary, tactic, particularly if your opponent has taken control of the game.

If your opponent has one of his balls near, but not over, a pocket it can give you the advantage to sneak one of your balls behind it and possibly force your opponent to pot your ball, thus committing a foul.

In nine-ball a pocket blocker is much less effective, because a player can always pot it providing they hit the lowest numbered ball available first.

You will on occasion find yourself in a game that is being decided by the

Covering Pockets

Leaving a ball over the pocket is a very useful tactic. A clearance won't be available every time, and you mustn't get caught up in the idea that you always need to clear all the balls from the table. You can buy yourself some time with this tactic, especially if your opponent has the advantage in a game.

final ball, but you face a difficult shot to try to pot it. To attempt a pot can sometimes prove to be a mistake, since the ball could easily end up in the jaws of a pocket. Sometimes it would be more sensible to play a containing safety shot.

This could simply be to hit the object ball tight onto a side rail, forcing your opponent into making an extremely difficult bank shot to win. If the ball is tight against a rail and you don't fancy a tough shot to pot it, given the good chance that the ball will end up in the jaws of the pocket if you miss, it might be advisable to simply play the ball around the angles and try to put it in a safe position. Again, you should try to maximize the distance between cue ball and object ball.

The chances are that you will be nervous and tense at such a key stage of a game, but you should always remember that all of the initial skills that you have learned can be of great use; the ability to judge angles off a rail, playing the shot at a particular pace, and hitting the object ball in the correct place.

When Not to Pot

131

Knowing the Rules

You should always make sure that you know the rules of the game before you play (see page 206). Some of them will be extremely familiar to you, but others can take more time to fully understand because they are more complicated.

The push-out rule is one that needs to be remembered for nine-ball pool, with players sometimes taking the option to push the cue ball to an awkward position with their shot immediately after a break, knowing the cue ball doesn't have to make contact either with another ball or a rail. A player should always tell their opponent when they are going to be playing this shot. You should also bear in mind that you are allowed to put your opponent back in to play after their push-out shot. You don't have to play from that awkward position if you don't want to.

Having spent many years marveling and despairing in equal measure at how "house rules" can change from bar to bar, I know how important it is to establish the rules before a game. This means that you should not only be clear about the rules in your head, but establish whether your opponent is too, especially on the basic rules. It might be useful to carry with you some of the main rules printed out, especially if you are playing in a competition. And if you are playing the game in another country, you should be aware that the rules can be very different to those that you are used to at home.

FOULS

You should remember that in nine-ball pool three consecutive fouls lose the game, and if you or your opponent happen to have made two it would be better to establish before the third that you are both aware of the situation. You should keep an eye on all the balls from every shot, remembering that one has to make contact with a rail if no ball is potted.

If you are playing some forms of the game, including eight-ball, one rule that can catch many players out is the deliberate foul, which some do use to their advantage. Players can make a deliberate foul at any time and without warning their opponent. The shot is often played to deliberately pot an opponent's ball that is over a pocket, leaving that pocket clear. It is less common in nine-ball but will sometimes be considered when a player finds they are snookered, with little prospect of making an escape. Another ball may be hit into an awkward position, often into a cluster of other balls, making it difficult for the opponent to run out in the game.

Anybody that has played this game for any reasonable period of time will quickly identify with the frustrations that often arise from pool rules. This is largely because they have differed for so long within various bodies and organizations, and it hasn't always been easy to establish consistency across the board.

If you are playing blackball, you should also be aware of the two shot-rule after a foul has been made, giving you the chance to play one shot without potting a ball and still stay at the table. In nine-ball, you only have one shot at the table if your opponent has fouled, but you have ball in hand, meaning that you can move the cue ball anywhere on the table. In eight-ball, the rules also allow for ball in hand after any foul, but you will find many casual players placing the cue ball behind the head string after a foul has been committed.

Many players are caught out by the free-ball rule that is often used in eight-ball and blackball. This rule establishes that if your opponent has fouled, and you are unable to see both sides of any of your object balls, you could nominate to pot one of your opponent's balls as your own, and still continue with your inning. This can be especially useful to you if an opponent's ball is blocking the pocket, preventing you from pocketing any of your balls into it.

TRUSTING YOUR OPPONENT

Sometimes, we can all get so caught up in our own game that we forget our opponent. It should be said that the vast majority of people that play the game are extremely honest, and want nothing more than a fair and friendly game. Indeed, one of the great traditions of pool is its inherent honesty. Players will call themselves after making a foul, even if it wasn't really possible for the other player to spot it.

However, it is worth keeping an eye on an opponent's shots, just in case you are unfortunate enough to be playing somebody not quite as keenly aware of the honest traditions of pool as you are.

Read up on the rules to check anything you are unsure of. They are widely documented these days, with the World Pool-Billiard Association a good place to start when checking for official rules (see page 206). You shouldn't get too bogged down by the rules though, for fear of spoiling your enjoyment of the game.

The Mental Game

One television commentator has always begun his stint behind the microphone at the World Snooker Championships with the words "And here begins the 17-day marathon of the mind." It is a phrase that can sum up all cue sports nicely. As with so many sports, pool is as much a test of mental strength as potting ability. A leading young British player told me how agonizing it is to sit and watch your opponent clear the balls.

This is where pool differs from so many other sports. In football, a player can make a mistake that might lead to a touchdown, and that could be absolutely crucial in a game. The chances are, however, that there will be time left to change the game, and that individual can still have some bearing on the outcome, while playing as part of a team. In another one-on-one sport, tennis, players will regularly make mistakes but this will only ever lose them one point. They can put their mistake right by playing well in the next point.

Pool does not allow such luxuries. If a mistake is made, you can lose the game, watching helplessly as your opponent takes advantage of it to clear the balls from the table. It is easy to suggest you must stay positive at all times, but staying positive is indeed essential—you must always feel confident enough in your own abilities to play a good shot next time.

Think Positive

If negative thoughts begin to take over, your game will suffer as a result. There is no doubt that one of the biggest battles you will face in this game is the battle in your own head. You should try to remember that you can't change anything that has already happened in a game, and can only affect what is going to happen in the future. You should try to forget any mistake that has been made as quickly as possible, and remember the good parts of your game. If you find yourself getting weighed down by mistakes, this will adversely affect your game.

Mental strength as well as technique is essential in pool.

The Mental Game

Dealing with Mistakes

Dwelling on past mistakes is something we can all do, in life as well as in pool. This is exacerbated in pool, because very often you have to just sit back and watch while your opponent sinks the balls. It can seem as if they are pouring salt on the wounds.

There is an opportunity with each shot in a game of pool to weigh up the options. You have time to think about the shot, and judge the best way to play it. This will not always be the case in other sports. If a football player has an opponent steaming toward them, or a tennis player is faced

with a ball smashed toward their body, the judgment has to be instant. In those situations, the players will often be relying on instinct.

But in pool, players have that little bit longer to consider the most appropriate shot to play in the circumstances. Sometimes, however, we will play the wrong shot. It happens to all players of all levels. On occasion, although it should be strongly discouraged, there will be a nagging doubt in the back of the mind while you are playing a shot.

This could be the case if you are attempting a difficult pot. There will be a voice somewhere telling you to play safe. If you miss the shot, and leave your opponent with a good chance, the

1978

A huge television audience of 11 million tunes in to watch a classic grudge-match between pool legends Willie Mosconi and Rudolf Walter Wanderone Junior.

knowledge that you were considering playing a different shot can make the disappointment greater.

When you reach a certain level, you must trust your game and your judgment. As with anything, experience will be invaluable. The more you play the game, the more you will be able to focus on putting mistakes behind you.

It should be remembered that none of us are machines, and sometimes in a game of pool we will make the wrong choices, or even just play a bad shot. The best players will be able to put that mistake behind them as soon as possible. Some will put it behind them immediately, and focus on making a better choice next time.

Luck

Sometimes, you will find yourself undone by one of the most mysterious commodities in all of life. I'm talking about one simple four-letter word—luck. You can have all the coaching in the world, and have been improving rapidly over a period of time. You feel confident enough to take on a decent player, and beat them.

You may find yourself in a promising position in a particular game, and then suddenly it all changes in an instant. You may have made good contact with the cue ball, but the object ball has jumped in the air, through no fault of your own. Your opponent could have hit a ball toward a pocket, watched it miss and bounce away from the jaws, only to creep along the foot rail and into the opposite corner

pocket. It could be a moment that changes the game, or even wins the game.

Sometimes, luck truly will favor the brave in a game of pool, or those players that tend to play more aggressive shots. If a player plays as controlled a shot as possible into a cluster of balls, using power, and their intended object ball drops in, you could argue that they deserve their piece of fortune for playing an aggressive shot, and making things happen.

Another player could hit the cue ball with medium pace into the same cluster, with their main intention being not to greatly disturb any of the balls. It is obviously far more unlikely that any ball will drop into the pocket. In this instance, a player could be said to have made their own luck.

Jordan Church

Trusting to Luck

Luck is simply part of the game, and always will be. It's happened before that a piece of luck has gone against me, and cost me a match—however the opposite has also been true. You should try to keep your composure at all times. If necessary, you can take a quick break between games.

Confidence in your game and taking chances can pay off.

Be Prepared

If you start to reach a decent level with your game, it can't be emphasized enough how important preparation is. You should spend time practicing your shots before a game. By now, the basics of the game will be second nature; your stance, bridge hand, and how you hold the cue will become as normal to you as walking down the street. But there will never be any harm in trying out various shots, using draw and English to control the cue ball. Practice a dozen bank shots, or maybe judging the angles off a rail to try to escape from a snooker. If you are feeling well prepared, it will boost your confidence ready for any game. Remember that each game of pool is different, and that you never know when you will need to call on your various skills.

1979

The American Poolplayers Association (APA) is founded by professional players Terry Bell and Larry Hubbart. It was originally known as the National Pool League, until it became the APA in 1981. The Association has nearly 300,000 members.

You may find that some people state they haven't played for a while before starting a game of pool (you may want to turn this into a joke, and ask if they are a hustler!). There is nothing impressive about this if it is true, and any good player will admit they always feel more confident if they have had plenty of practice.

You should try to check the table before you start a game; check the quality of the cloth and the state of the rails. You should hit the cue ball toward the rails on a couple of occasions, to see if it bounces off normally. If you are playing a match of semi-importance, in a bar league or local competition, you might want to check with your opponent to make sure they are happy with the table.

If you both find there are parts of the table that aren't to your satisfaction, you should consider moving to play on a different one if this is possible. It is important that you are able to focus on your own game and qualities, and not worry about the state of the table you are playing on.

Know Your Opponent

It is important first and foremost to concentrate on your own game, but, as I said earlier, you should always keep a keen eye on your opponent as well. You should try to judge the quality of their game, and identify any possible weaknesses that they are showing.

Obviously if you are playing somebody on a regular basis, you will know their game pretty well. But if you are playing in a competition and taking on somebody you haven't previously seen, their skills will be an unknown to you. They may dazzle early on with the quality of their potting, but you shouldn't become disheartened by this. Sometimes you will find that their tactical or safety play isn't of a sufficient quality to beat your game.

It isn't a crime to play a negative safety shot when the occasion demands, perhaps electing to hit the object ball into a cluster of other balls, making it almost impossible to pot. You should try to force your opponent into making a mistake, perhaps into committing a foul and giving you ball in hand.

Similarly, if your opponent seems to be adopting a more negative approach, you could do worse than trying some ambitious pots. If somebody is playing cautious shots, it could be because they are not feeling especially confident, and this can be something you can take advantage of.

If your opponent has already missed one or two potting opportunities, it might be sensible to leave them a couple of tempters from distance. You should always be weighing up the percentages, trying to judge whether you think your opponent is likely to make a particular shot. You should be aware that as much as you are keeping an eye on your opponent, they will also be keeping an eye on you. Again, it is important to appear confident and positive—you can be sure that any obvious signs of disappointment or frustration will boost your opponent's confidence.

If your opponent seems to be particularly attacking in their approach, you might want to consider adopting a more tactical, cautious approach in order to frustrate them.

Mental Discipline

Clearly, your reactions during a game of pool will sometimes be a reflection of your general character. A more positive person is likely to back themselves more often to successfully make a shot, even if they have recently missed. A person who is prone to pessimistic thoughts must train themselves as best they can to remain upbeat about their chances.

You must never openly display your frustration or anger. You may not have won a game in a long time, or may have missed a number of good chances in succession. It seems to be true that when you are playing well, and with confidence, the pockets are like buckets, with balls dropping in everywhere. The opposite can also be the case, with the pockets seeming to close up and balls constantly hitting the jaws rather than dropping.

Sometimes, it can simply be a matter of concentration. When things aren't going well, it can be natural to let the mind drift. You should always try to ensure this doesn't happen.

It sometimes needs only one piece of poor judgment for you to lose the game. If you aren't fully concentrating, the obvious can be missed. We have all been in situations where we have been too quick to play the shot, and only afterward noticed another ball—it is too late then to ask: "Why didn't I hit that other ball?" Try to maintain your levels of concentration from the first shot to the last.

Tactical Play

There will always be a place in pool for frustrating your opponent. Sometimes, the balls can be in awkward positions, and a long, tactical, game is the only option. When involved in one of these games, you should think of a situation you wouldn't like to find yourself in, and leave your opponent in exactly that situation. Some people feel that they should play to their opponent's weaknesses, but I've always felt the best advice is to play to your own strengths.

Concentrate on your game rather than your opponent.

Mental Discipline

Challenging Yourself

Whatever level of the game you are playing at, you should be having fun. If you find that you never seem to have fun, you may be playing the wrong game. However, if you find that you are regularly beating other people in your local bar, you should think about trying to better your game at a higher level.

Challenging yourself will help you improve your game.

As with any pursuit, you want to feel that you are being tested to your limits. Your own game would soon become stale if you were only playing people much worse than yourself. If you play predominantly in a bar, it might be sensible to find your nearest pool hall and play there. Generally speaking, those that play in pool halls play to a higher level than your average player in a bar.

I once heard a radio DJ say that "tennis is like malice." This is an odd phrase, but one that basically means it is more fun to play a game or have an argument with somebody of equal skills or intellect. The same is true of pool—it might seem like fun at first, but we would all soon become exceedingly bored by winning matches easily.

You might also want to join a local league or play in competitions. It might be a baptism of fire at first, discovering that there are indeed lots of people out there who are pretty handy at playing this game, but in time it can only be good for you and the development of your game.

As I mentioned earlier, you should try to catch the professionals playing a game, maybe live or more likely on television. Study the way they play certain shots, and try to gauge how far ahead they are thinking. The truth is that they are usually thinking about potting the final ball throughout the whole game, and you will want to adopt a similar mindset as you improve your skills.

Trying Other Games

You could consider trying out a different version of pool or even a different cue sport, because sometimes a person's particular talents can lend themselves well to a certain form of pool, or a different game altogether.

1986

The Color of Money, a sequel to *The Hustler*, is released. Paul Newman is in the same role, with Tom Cruise co-starring as an up-and-coming professional. The film helped to bring the game to a new generation.

If you find that you enjoy the tactical form of the game, nine-ball may not be your first choice of game, since it still relies largely on attacking play and potting. One-pocket remains a popular version of pool in some places. The object of this game is to score points by pocketing balls into specific, designated pockets, with victory achieved when you have scored an agreed number of points—most commonly eight.

The player making the break shot will choose a foot corner pocket, which they must stick with for the rest of the game. The other player must pocket their balls in the other foot corner pocket. Often these games can be long and drawn-out, and require careful planning and tactical play. Sometimes you will play shots in such a way as to prevent your opponent scoring points, perhaps caroming one of their balls away from the chosen pocket. Trying to negotiate your balls into positions from which they can be pocketed can often require patience and skill. If you are a more attacking player, you might want to experiment with some of the spin-offs from nine-ball pool. These include six-ball, which is essentially the same game as nine-ball but with three fewer balls, and seven-ball, where the balls are set up in an unusual hexagonal rack.

Ten-ball is popular with some players, because you can't pocket the final ball early in the game for an early win, as you can in nine-ball. It is therefore seen by some as more challenging, and a game in which players can show off their safety game and tactical play. There has been talk in the professional ranks in recent years of replacing nine-ball with ten-ball at the highest level.

Another form of the game that has been gaining popularity in recent years is bank pool. This is played with 15 or 9 balls, but they are not racked in any particular order. The winner is the player who pots 8 balls (or 5 balls if played with a smaller rack) with bank shots.

Many pool halls will allow you to play these variant games, and will have the necessary balls, but the two forms of pool that remain by far the most popular around the world are nine-ball and eight-ball.

Playing Snooker

Some players simply find that in time they are better suited to a much bigger table and the different tests it provides. If you find yourself falling into that category, you may want to try out snooker.

It will take you some time to get used to the much bigger playing surface, and the different skills you will have to use. Many shots require a lot more pace than you have used on a pool table, and you often have to work much harder at controlling the cue ball.

The same principles still apply, however, from the basics of addressing the shot correctly, to judging the angles and using the rails to your advantage. Games of snooker naturally last much longer than pool games, and concentration levels need to be maintained throughout.

Generally speaking, particularly when players are starting out or still inexperienced, a single mistake won't be too costly. It may cost a player a few points, but these can be made up over the course of a game. Many players relish the long passages of safety play that can sometimes take place, with pots sometimes too difficult to attempt and more advantage to be gained from leaving your opponent in an awkward position on the table.

The game is played with 15 red balls, each worth 1 point to pot, and 6 colored balls. These range in value from the yellow ball, worth 2 points, to the black ball, which

1990
The first World Nine-Ball Championship is held in Germany. The event is won superbly by the charismatic and popular American star Earl Strickland.

is worth 7. After every red, you must attempt to pot a color, which is then placed back on the table on its own spot if potted. When all the reds have been cleared from the table, you must pot the colors in order, starting with the yellow and finishing with the black.

To achieve victory, you simply need to score more points than your opponent. Sometimes the game will only be won by potting the final black ball, but more often than not a player will be more points ahead than the value of points left on the table.

Playing snooker requires careful thinking and planning, extremely accurate cueing, and an ability to play good safety shots. You might want to try it out, not least because when you return to playing pool afterward you should find the experience has improved your game.

Some people play on a half-size table, but for the full, authentic experience you should try to play on a full-size table. These usually measure 12 ft by 6 ft and, generally speaking, are covered with a cloth of green baize, which will include a nap.

Playing Billiards

The game of pool is known to have derived from billiards, but that game isn't common today. It is still played in certain parts of the world however, and is quite different from pool. It is fair to say that billiards does have a rather old-fashioned image, but the game does still retain its fascination, even for those of us that have rarely played it.

Carom billiards is today most commonly played in Asia and South America. It is played on pocketless tables, normally the same size as a pool table, with one object ball and two cue balls. The object of the game is to hit both the opponent's cue ball and object ball in the same shot. It is a game that will seriously test your ability to judge angles, and requires accuracy and concentration. The game moves at a much slower pace than pool, and maybe that is why it doesn't appeal to many in today's fast-paced world.

Sean Connery enjoys a game of bar billiards at his basement flat in London, 1962.

Gospel according to...

Jordan Church

Transferable Skills

Transferring skills between different cue sports can be difficult at times, because bad habits in one game can be useful habits in another. You should try and keep it as simple as possible when you first try another game, trusting the skills you have already picked up.

If you're particularly lucky, you may see the game of bar billiards played in the United Kingdom, but it will be a rare sighting. The game is played on a small table, without corner or side pockets, but with nine holes. There are seven white balls and a red ball, and points are scored by hitting the balls into the holes.

In the United Kingdom, you will occasionally see people playing English billiards. This is played on a full-size table, with pockets, measuring 12 ft by 6 ft. In this game, points can be scored by both caroming your opponent's cue ball and the object ball, and by potting balls—sometimes players will do both in the same shot.

The different games on offer are testament to the sheer enjoyment that can be gained from playing cue sports. You should consider trying out one or more of these games, being aware that even if you don't stick with them in the long term, they won't do any harm to your skills on the pool table.

Playing Billiards

155

Chapter Five:
TRICK SHOTS

Trick shots have proved to be one of the most popular features of the game of pool. Many top players enjoy entertaining crowds with their favorite one. Have a look at some of the classics...

Trick shots are skillful and extremely impressive. They can be mastered through practice and perseverance.

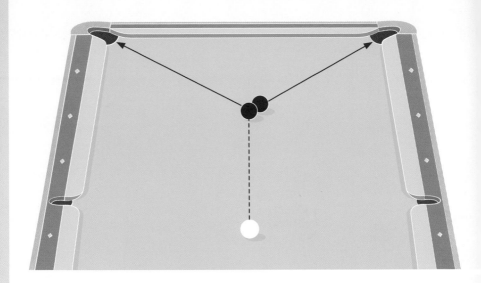

You should line up two red balls with the black spot in the middle. The balls should line up so that they would make a plant in both the corner and center pockets. You should aim to hit the first ball full in the face, and both balls should disappear into opposite corner pockets.

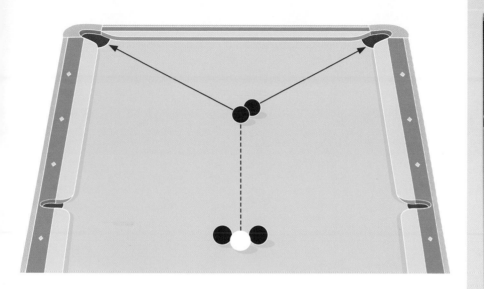

You should place two red balls in the same position as in the previous shot. The other two balls should be touching the cue ball and facing opposite center pockets. You should push through the cue ball with strong pace, and the first two balls should disappear into the center pockets, with the other two balls potted into the corner pockets.

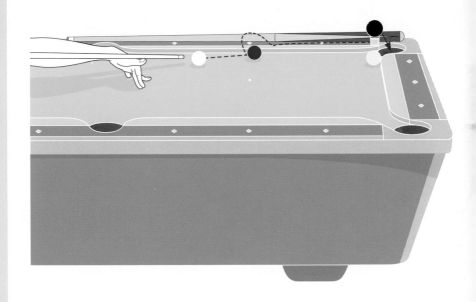

You should raise your cue and bridge hand. You should strike the top of the cue ball, enabling it to jump after making connection with the red ball. The cue ball will then be guided by the cue along the top of the side rail and knock the black off the top of the chalk and into the pocket.

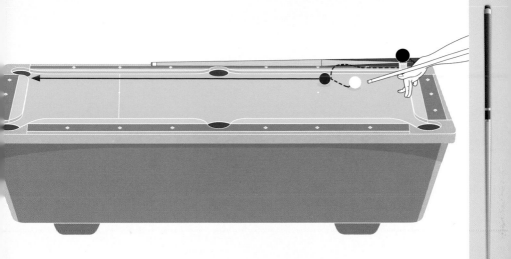

This is a similar shot to before, and has to be hit very accurately. You should raise your cue and bridge hand again, but this time aim for the bottom of the cue ball. You can pot the red and jump the cue ball on to the side rail, again knocking the black off the chalk and into the pocket.

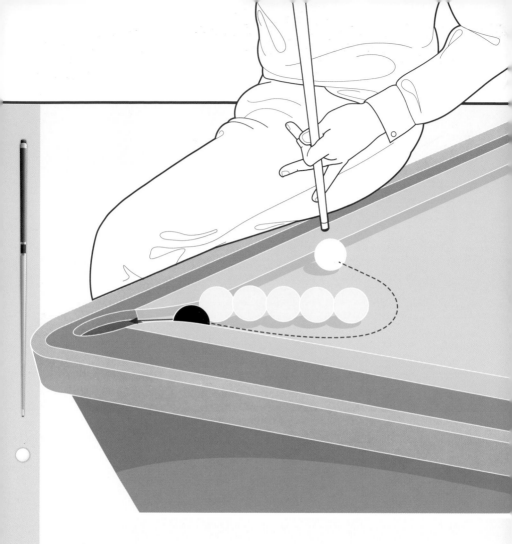

You should sit on the rail and rest the bridge hand on your leg. Raise the cue to a 90-degree angle, and strike the top of the cue ball at the point closest to you. This will create enough spin to bend the cue ball around the five yellow balls and pot the black.

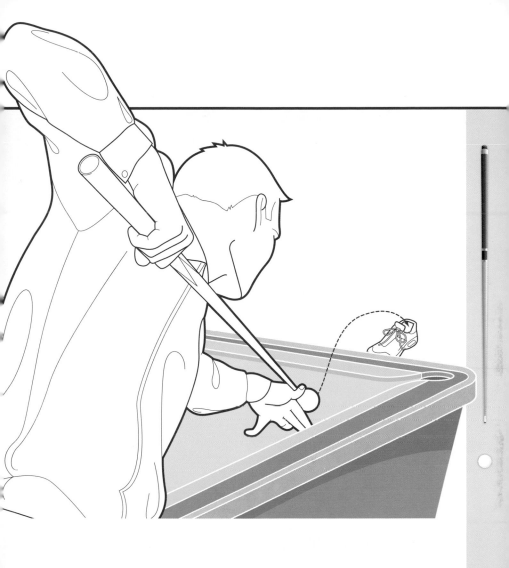

You should place a shoe on the floor around 5 feet away from the table. You need to raise your cue to around 45 degrees, hitting the cue ball with considerable pace. It should jump off the table, and you will need to judge the pace necessary for the cue ball to fall into the shoe.

This shot requires good touch, and you will
need to raise your cue to an angle of around 45
degrees. You need to aim for the bottom of the
black ball, hitting the cue ball on its left-hand
side. The black should jump into the space inside
the triangle.

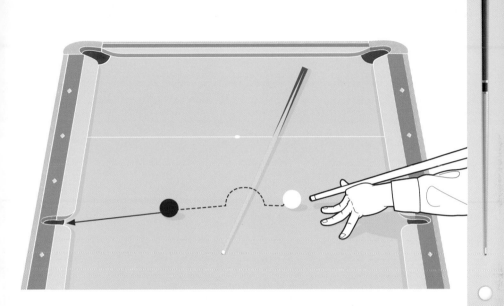

You should line up the cue ball and red ball as if you were playing a simple shot into the center pocket, and place a cue between them. You should slightly raise the cue, and strike down on the cue ball at firm pace. It should jump over the cue and pot the red.

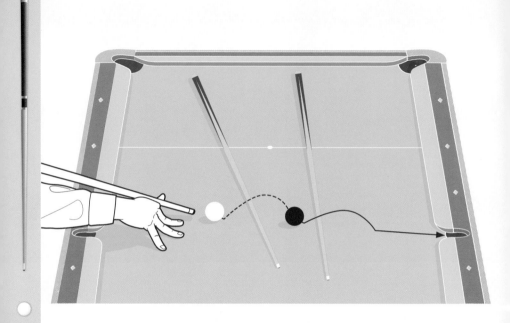

You should slightly raise the cue and bridge hand for this shot. You will need to hit this with enough pace to clear both cues. You should strike down on the cue ball in order for it to clear the first cue and connect with the top of the red. You are aiming to pot the red.

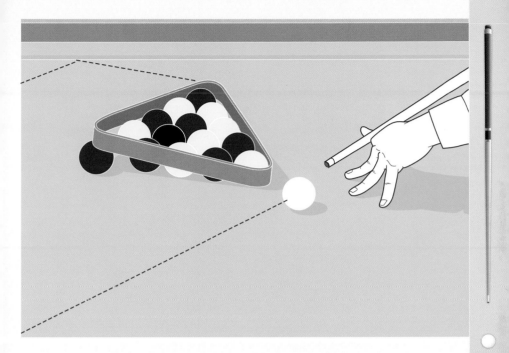

You need to judge your angles perfectly off the rails for this shot. You will aim to hit one side rail, the foot rail, and then the other side rail with the cue ball. You should play the shot with enough pace for the cue ball to clip the triangle and knock the red into place.

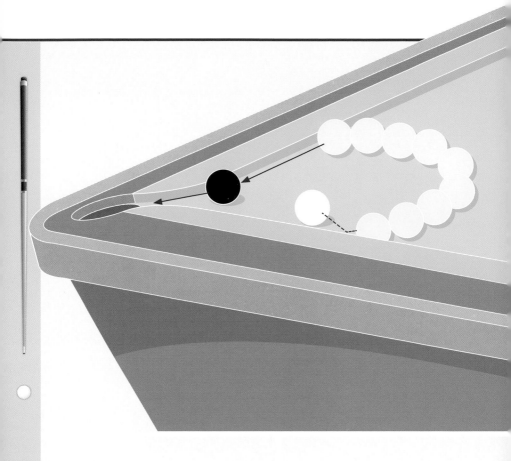

You should hold the cue in its normal position for this shot. You should hit the cue ball into the rail with some left-hand English. If the shot is played correctly, the cue ball should clip the first yellow ball, with a knock-on effect on all the other yellow balls, before potting the black.

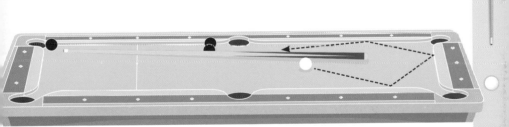

This shot will test your judgment of angles, with the cue ball needing to be struck against one side rail, and then connect with the foot rail and side rail nearest the cue. The cue ball will then push the cue away and head toward the corner pocket, potting the red.

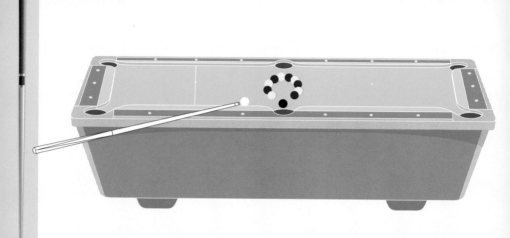

This shot needs to be hit with the right amount of pace. Ten balls should be lined up in an extravagant plant, in the shape of a horseshoe. There needs to be a gap between those balls and the black on the pocket. If the shot is played accurately, the black should be potted.

This shot looks particularly impressive if it works out. You should hit the ball nearest to the cue ball, which is near the rail. The black will bounce out and toward the corner pocket. If it has sufficient pace, the black will jump through the triangle and over the yellow balls, into the pocket.

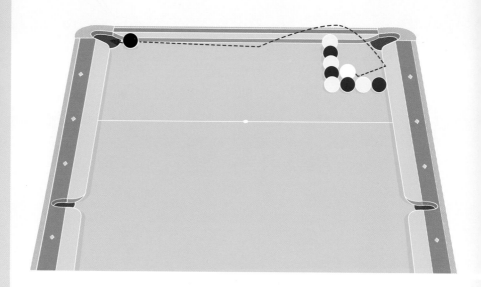

You need to slightly raise the cue for this shot and strike down on the cue ball against the side rail, as if you were playing a bank shot to the opposite corner pocket. The cue ball should bounce off the side rail and over the balls to pot the black.

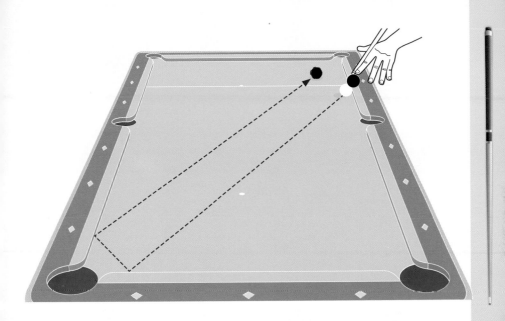

You should place your bridge hand carefully on the side rail, and hit the cue ball toward the head rail and then the side rail. If the cue ball is hit with accuracy and the right pace it will connect with the black ball on the way back, which has been knocked onto the table, and pot it.

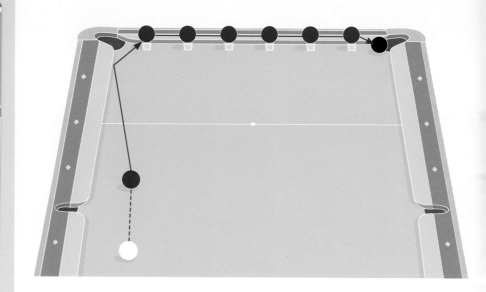

You should hit the red ball toward the corner pocket, but aim for it to hit the side rail just before the pocket. The red should then connect with the first red placedon chalk, which will be knocked off. A domino effect should then be created, with the final red pushing the black into the pocket.

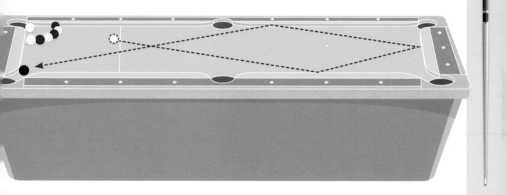

You should place six balls in front of the cue ball, which is placed against the jaw of a corner pocket. You should raise your cue and play a jump shot, aiming to make the cue ball bounce off three rails to pot the black. For an even tougher shot you should strike down on the center of the cue ball against the other jaw, making it jump and producing the same outcome.

Chapter Six:
THE GREATS
OF THE GAME

The greatest players to have graced
the game of pool in the past century
have delighted spectators with their
talent and skills. We remember
some of the greats of yesteryear
and today, and also feature some of
the sport's biggest tournaments.

So many of the past great players influence those who wish to become well known and admired.

Ralph Greenleaf

The game of pool has been blessed with an array of outstanding talent down the years. So many great champions have thrilled spectators with their skills, and have consistently raised the standards of the sport.

One of the first great champions of pool was Ralph Greenleaf. Hailing from Monmouth, Illinois, Greenleaf totally dominated the sport for many years, winning 20 world titles. He was a charismatic figure, who is rightly credited with helping to bring the sport to a wider audience in its early days.

He won his first world title in 1919, and then kept on winning it until a 20th success in 1937. Like most of pool's early stars, Greenleaf played the game of 14.1, and once recorded a high run of 126. He stunned spectators with a brilliant high single-game average of 63 in 1929.

Not only was Greenleaf a brilliant player on the table, he was a colorful character off it. He married vaudeville actress Amelia Ruth Parker, who was known by the stage names "Princess Nai Tai" and "The Oriental Nightingale." He was widely known to have battled for many years with alcoholism. The press labeled him as one of sport's early "playboys," and in 1935 newspapers were full of sensational headlines when it was reported that Greenleaf "fell off the wagon" when he

1994

The Mosconi Cup, an annual competition between teams from Europe and the United States, takes place for the first time in Romford, England. The USA wins the event 16–12.

vanished just before a crucial tournament in New York and woke up in Oklahoma under arrest as a vagrant.

After he died at the age of just 50 in 1950, the *New York Times'* obituary left the reader in no doubt as to his importance and significance to the game of pool.

"What Babe Ruth did for baseball, Dempsey did for fighting, Tilden did for tennis... Greenleaf did for pocket billiards."

To be compared to the legendary Babe Ruth is high praise indeed. Greenleaf will always be remembered as a true legend of the sport.

Ralph Greenleaf was one of the first three players to be inducted into the Billiard Congress of America's Hall of Fame in 1966.

Willie Mosconi

No discussion about the greats of pool could ever properly take place without mentioning Willie Mosconi. A true legend of the game, Mosconi was the most talked-about figure in pool for a generation and his contribution in helping to popularize it as a national recreational activity is immeasurable.

Born in 1913, Mosconi was already displaying brilliant cue talents by the age of six, leading Greenleaf to forecast (after playing him in an exhibition match) that he would one day be world champion. He duly won the BCA's World Championship an amazing 15 times between 1941 and 1957. In a match against Arthur Cranfield in 1945 he enjoyed a best high run of 127.

Mosconi also played the 14.1 form of the game, and he still holds the officially recognized high run record of 526 consecutive balls. Mosconi produced his amazing run on an 8 ft by 4 ft Brunswick pool table in Springfield, Ohio, in 1954. He also played many hundreds of exhibition matches during his life, particularly after his retirement, where he often delighted crowds with his extensive array of trick shots.

Breaking

The break shot will often contain elements of luck, but you can help yourself by hitting the cue ball just above its center, ideally making it stop somewhere near the middle of the table. Accidentally potting the cue ball, particularly in the center pockets, should be avoided at all costs.

Mosconi always remained part of public consciousness, even in his later years. He played the part of a sportscaster in the 1980 film *The Baltimore Bullet*, starring James Coburn and Omar Sharif, and also appeared in the music video for George Thorogood's 1982 hit "Bad to the Bone." He played his last challenge match against Jimmy Caras at the Valley Billiards Hall of Fame tribute show in 1991.

Mosconi died in 1993 at the age of 80, but his contribution to the game of pool will not quickly be forgotten. A year after his death, the Mosconi Cup, an annual pool competition between American and European players, was founded in his honor.

Mosconi (pictured above on set with Paul Newman) was the technical advisor on the 1961 movie *The Hustler*, with his job being to teach Paul Newman how to walk, talk, and play like a real hustler.

Willie Mosconi

Irving Crane & Steve Mizerak

Irving Crane will go down as an all-time great of the game. Crane also excelled in 14.1, or continuous pool, and won six world titles. He was nicknamed "The Deacon," due to his gentlemanly ways, his very cautious approach to the game, and his impeccable suits.

He learned the game at home as a young boy, after his mother replaced a dining table with an 8 ft by 4 ft pool table. He once said in later life: "Other kids, you know, they'd play for 20 minutes or half an hour and they'd say, 'let's do something else.' I could play all day and never get enough. I couldn't wait to get home from school to play."

The longevity of his career was hugely impressive. He won his first world crown in 1946, and his final title in 1972. He once pocketed 309 successive balls during a charity match in Utah in 1939. His magnificent skills around the table delighted generations, and he was inducted into the BCA's hall of fame in 1978. In 1999 he was ranked as number eight on *Billiard Digest's* 50 greatest players of the century.

Mizerak became a well-known figure to the wider population when he appeared in a commercial for Miller Lite beer, and then later he starred in *The Color of Money*, the 1986 follow-up movie to *The Hustler.*

Steve Mizerak excelled in a brilliant career at the highest level. Mizerak won a host of big tournaments in the 1970s and 1980s, including four successive US Open 14.1 Championships from 1970 to 1973. He also captured two World Open titles, and in 1978 won the US Open Nine-Ball Championships.

In later life, he owned a number of pool halls in the West Palm Beach and Lake Park areas of Florida. He founded the Senior Tour in 1996 for players aged 50 and over.

Irving Crane & Steve Mizerak

Rudolf Walter Wanderone Jr. & Luther Lassiter

Rudolf Walter Wanderone Jr. was one of pool's most colorful characters, and started playing the game at a very young age. He became a traveling pool hustler as a teenager, and also hustled servicemen during World War Two.

He became the most recognized pool player in the United States when he adopted the nickname "Minnesota Fats" from a character in the hit movie *The Hustler*. Jackie Gleason played the role of "Fats" in the film, supposedly the greatest pool player in America.

Wanderone had already acquired notoriety and a number of nicknames. These included "Triple-Smart Fats," "New York Fats," "Broadway Fats," and "Chicago Fats." He was better known as "New York Fats" when Walter Tevis's book *The Hustler* hit the shelves. Wanderone was initially said to be considering suing, believing the fictional character was based on him, but soon changed his mind when he realized how much money could be made. It should be noted that Tevis always denied that the character was based on Wanderone.

After the success of the movie, Wanderone made a fine career for himself on television and in exhibitions. He played himself in a 1970 film *The Player* and appeared with Johnny Carson on his legendary chat show, as well as making an appearance in Britain on the David Frost show.

Wanderone also enjoyed promoting a feud with Willie Mosconi over how to best showcase the game. Wanderone believed it should be a rough-and-tumble gambling game, but Mosconi saw it as a genteel and skillful pastime. The two famously clashed on ABC's *Wide World of Sports* in 1978 in a match watched by almost 11 million viewers. Only the boxing rematch between Muhammad Ali and Leon Spinks attracted a bigger audience to the show that year.

Mosconi won the game, but Wanderone was definitely the crowd favorite with his easy humor and banter. Wanderone joined the hall of fame in 1984, and to this day his name is legendary in the game.

One of Walderone's great hustling friends was Luther Lassiter, who proved himself to be one of the truly great players in a long career. Known by anybody and everybody as "Wimpy," Lassiter was at one time the "undisputed king of the hustlers," reportedly winning over $300,000 from gambling on pool games between 1942 and 1948.

He would take on, and beat, a number of pool greats during his career, and he was also one of the first to really excel in the game of nine-ball. He still played widely after his retirement, including twice in the "The Legendary Stars of Pocket Billiards Tournament" in Atlantic City in the 1980s.

Like all men at the top of this game, Lassiter could never have been said to be short on confidence. He was once reported to have said: "I watch a man shoot pool for an hour. If he misses more than one shot I know I can beat him."

Rudolf Walter Wanderone Jr. (pictured above) became known throughout the pool world and beyond as "Minnesota Fats." Wanderone was a legendary hustler, and a hugely charismatic figure who delighted crowds wherever he played.

Jim Rempe, James "Cisero" Murphy & Ray Martin

Jim Rempe enjoyed a long and distinguished run at the top of the sport, particularly in the 1970s. He was so dominant at one stage, winning 23 tournaments between 1972 and 1978, that he was given the nickname "King James."

In a brilliant career, Rempe claimed over 100 major championships. He won 11 world titles, including the World Straight Ball Championship and World Nine-Ball title. He has still been competing in recent years, often in invitational events with some of the other all-time greats of the game. He has also branched out into product development and marketing, with his Jim Rempe Training

Nicknamed "King James," Jim Rempe began playing pool at the age of 6 and turned pro aged 22 years old.

Ball. This is basically a cue ball marked with rings and targets to help players with cue ball control. It has proved to be quite a success with players of all ages and standards.

James "Cisero" Murphy, from Brooklyn, was the first top African-American player to break into the big time. He became City Champion in 1953 and State Champion in 1958, but couldn't compete in world title events for many years due to the racial tensions at the time. Many players picketed outside the front of the Commodore Hotel in Burbank, California, to protest at his exclusion. When the battle was eventually won and he was allowed to compete, Murphy triumphed convincingly, winning the Burbank World Invitational 14.1 tournament in 1965.

In his later years, Murphy was at the forefront of various city programs that aimed to help young adults and children. He would visit veterans' hospitals, senior citizens' homes, and mental hospitals giving trick shot exhibitions and teaching people how to play the game.

Ray Martin was another star who was very definitely from the "old school." He was known throughout the pool world as "Cool Cat," after he calmly won a world title in 1971 in California— during an earthquake.

He won the straight pool world title at his first attempt in 1971, and went on to win it twice more, in 1974 and 1978. Later in his career, Martin won a number of major nine-ball tournaments.

Cisero Murphy is one of two players to win the World Title on a first attempt, the other being Ray Martin.

Earl Strickland

Earl Strickland has probably been the greatest champion of the modern era, and certainly one of the sport's most colorful characters in the past couple of decades. He is widely regarded by pundits and fans as one of the best nine-ball players in the history of the sport.

Strickland rose to prominence with a major tournament victory in Lake Tahoe in 1983, and the following year he won his first US Open Nine-Ball Championships. From there, the victories and titles just kept on coming. He won the US Open title again, and then two successive World Nine-Ball Championship titles in 1990 and 1991.

He claimed three more US Open titles, making him the only man to win five, and won the World Championship title for the third time in 2002. Not before time, he was inducted into the BCA's Hall of Fame in 2006, and to the present day he remains one of the game's most feared competitors.

Jordan Church

English

The size of your tip can affect how the balls move after applying English. It is a difficult skill to master, and proficiency will only come with plenty of practice. Hitting a ball against the rail with English and aiming to pot it in an opposite pocket is a good way of developing the skill.

Despite his various infractions, Strickland remains a popular figure. Even when he is booed, the crowd are essentially just playing a game. The bottom line is that he is good for the sport—tournament organizers, his fellow players, and supporters all know it.

Nearly as famous as Strickland's triumphs on the table have been his various run-ins with fellow players and the authorities over the years. During an explosive clash with British snooker star Steve Davis at the World Championship in 2003, he used foul language and argued with fans and the referee.

During the 2007 Mosconi Cup, he had to be separated from English star Daryl Peach, with the obvious animosity between the pair threatening to turn into violence. At the 2008 Mosconi Cup, he argued with European fans in the crowd and swore during a live television interview. Strickland's reputation as one of the most unpredictable characters in pool was being cemented.

Earl Strickland

Efren Reyes, Francisco Bustamante & Daryl Peach

Efren Reyes, from the Philippines, is one of the truly great players of modern times. Often referred to as "The Magician," Reyes won the first World Nine-Ball Championship to be televised, when he claimed victory at the first event organized by Matchroom Sport in 1999.

He has won many major tournaments in eight-ball, nine-ball, and billiards, and some seasoned watchers have openly declared him to be the best to have ever played the game. A major star in his home country, Reyes was the first Asian player to be inducted into the BCA's Hall of Fame in 2003.

Francisco Bustamante, also from the Philippines,

1997

Germany's great pool champion Ralf Souquet receives the Silberne Lorbeerblatt (Silver Laurel Leaf), the highest official distinction awarded to sports stars in the country.

is one of the game's top international stars, having won a host of big titles in his career. Known for his graceful style at the table, Bustamante has won tournaments in eight-ball, nine-ball, and ten-ball.

He reached the final of the World Nine-Ball Championship in 2002, and his more recent victories have been in the World League in 2004, and the World Cup of Pool in 2006.

Daryl Peach made history when he became the first British player to win the World Nine-Ball Championship in 2007. Widely respected throughout the game, he made history by beating Roberto Gomez to win the title.

Nicknamed "Razzledazzle" and "The Dazzler," Peach was originally a snooker professional, but struggled to break into the world's top

Daryl Peach of England lines up a shot during the World Pool Championship held at the Araneta Coliseum in suburban Manila, 11 November 2007. Peach defeated Roberto Gomez of the Philippines 17–15 to take the championship.

200 and made the switch to pool. His big breakthrough win came with victory at the European Masters in 1995, and he has been mixing with the very best over the last decade.

During his controversial clash with Earl Strickland at the 2007 Mosconi Cup, the normally mild-mannered Peach referred to his opponent as "the scum of the Earth" in a post-match television interview.

Other Key Players

Gareth Potts (pictured on page 7) was always destined to reach the top from a young age. He won the Junior World Championships in 2000, and has since gone on to become a truly dominant figure in eight-ball pool.

He won the World Eight-Ball Federation's world title in 2005, 2007, and 2008 and has also claimed victory in a number of International tour events. Nicknamed "the Golden Boy," Potts has also been a regular for many years in the England team.

Chris Melling is another player who has tasted glory at the World Eight-Ball Championships, with victories in 2001 and 2003. Melling is not only a brilliant player, but one who plays the game at an incredibly quick

pace. He has attempted to break various speed records for potting balls.

Jason Twist won two World Championship titles in 2000 and 2002, and has since lost twice in the final. Another superb player who is known for his attacking style, Twist,

is nicknamed "The Tornado."

Quentin Hann is a former professional snooker player. He has often shown his brilliantly talented side on the pool table, winning the World Eight-Ball title in 1999.

Mark Selby has excelled at both snooker and pool. His finest moment came when he beat Darren Appleton to win the 2006 World Eight-Ball title. Selby also came within a whisker of being crowned world champion in snooker, losing in the 2007 final to John Higgins.

Carl Morris won the world title in 1998, and has won a host of titles all over the world. Thought of as a great role model in the game, his achievements are even more magnificent considering he was diagnosed as being profoundly deaf at the age of two. One of life's adventurers, Morris has helped to raise thousands of dollars for charity, on one occasion trekking across the Arctic to the North Pole.

Phil Harrison, another player who suffers from profound deafness, has also reached the very top of the game. He was developing something of a reputation for being a "nearly man" until his brilliant victory over Mick Hill to win the 2009 world title.

Quentin Hann (pictured left) has never been a stranger to controversy. He was banned from snooker for eight years after a British newspaper filmed him allegedly agreeing to lose a match on purpose in exchange for cash. Mark Selby (pictured below) has edged out Stephen Hendry, Stephen Maguire and Ken Doherty amoung others throughout his career.

Women

As is the case in so many sports, women have struggled to attain equality with their male counterparts, but there have been a number of notable players over the years.

Grandmother Dorothy Wise cleaned up many of the sport's big prizes after breaking through with victory in the women's division of the US Open Championship in 1967. She was the first female player to be inducted into the BCA's Hall of Fame.

Wise opened the door for many women to follow, and it was Jean Balukas who took up the baton. Balukas is known as a trailblazer in the sport, after years of rebelling against dress code and demanding to take on men in what was perceived to be their domain.

She won seven successive US Open titles from 1972 to 1978, dominating the sport in that decade. She won many other major titles, including six victories at the World Open Championships.

Toward the end of her career, she entered into competition alongside the men, and performed with great credit. At the 1987 BC Classic, a nine-ball event, she finished in ninth place.

Allison Fisher has written her name into the game's history books with her truly outstanding career. Fisher had already been dominant in the sport of snooker before traveling to the United States and trying her luck at professional pool in 1995. She won three successive

2005

The International Pool Tour is created. Closely modeled on golf's PGA Tour, top players have recently been battling it out for some of the largest prize funds in the sport's history.

World Championships in 1996, 1997, and 1998, and hasn't looked back since.

Her record is unmatched by anybody in the history of cue sports, and she has won more nine-ball tournaments than all her competitors combined. She won an amazing eight consecutive major professional tournaments in the 2000/2001 season. Known as a fine role model, Fisher has spent many years helping charities, and helping others to improve their game.

Sue Thompson has proved herself to be arguably the greatest of them all in eight-ball pool. She won her first world eight-ball title in 1996, and celebrated her ninth title with a superb victory in 2009. She is known for her quickfire, attacking style, which has made her one of the great entertainers as well as one of the great champions.

Jean Balukas played a number of legendary male players in specially arranged matches, including Willie Mosconi in CBS's "Challenge of the Sexes" in 1975. Despite having the advantage of a handicap and Mosconi playing at the age of 62, she made many sit up and take notice when she beat her illustrious opponent at both eight-ball and nine-ball. She is pictured here as a 6-year-old, performing in an exhibition in Grand Central Station, New York, in 1966.

The Mosconi Cup

The Mosconi Cup is an annual nine-ball tournament contested between teams representing Europe and the United States. The event has taken place every year since 1994, and was named in honor of American legend Willie Mosconi. It has been likened to golf's Ryder Cup, and attracts significant interest from sports fans on both sides of the Atlantic.

The event was staged in England for its first nine years, firstly taking place in the Essex towns of Romford, Basildon, and Dagenham. It was then moved to Bethnal Green in east London, where the event was staged for six successive years.

Since 2003, the Mosconi Cup has switched to a number of different locations, including Las Vegas and the Dutch towns of Egmond aan Zee and Rotterdam. In 2008, the event was held in the Maltese town of St. Julians.

Many of the great names have featured in the tournament over the years, including Earl Strickland and Johnny Archer. The event has attracted particular interest in the United Kingdom, where it is televised live by the satellite channel Sky.

To help sell the Mosconi Cup to viewers in Britain, a number of famous snooker stars played in the event in its early days. Among those that played were six-times world champion Steve Davis, the charismatic and brilliant Ronnie O'Sullivan, and Jimmy White, probably the most popular player in the history of snooker.

At first, the event seemed like more of an exhibition used to showcase the sport, but as the years have gone on it has developed into a much more serious and professional tournament, with snooker players tending not to take part and participation earned through invitation only (based on performances at other events).

The United States have mostly been dominant in the event, although Europe has enjoyed more success in recent times. Of the first 16 events, the USA won eleven and Europe four, with one match being tied. In 2009, the USA won the Mosconi Cup with an 11–7 victory in Las Vegas.

The Mosconi Cup has become well known for the partisan crowds and fervor it generates. With this passionate atmosphere have come the inevitable flashpoints, with the tension and excitement at times spreading to the players as well as the supporters.

The World Nine-Ball Championship

The World Nine-Ball Championship is one of the biggest events in the game of pool. The last two decades of competition have produced much drama and many great champions.

2009
China's Liu Sha-Sha wins the Women's World Nine-Ball Championship title, with victory over Ireland's Karen Corr in the Chinese city of Shenyang.

The event was first held in Bergheim, Germany, in 1990, and was won by Earl Strickland. The following two tournaments were staged in Las Vegas and Taipei, to further emphasize the truly international nature of this sport. Among the other early winners were Johnny Archer, who twice won in the 1990s, Oliver Ortmann, and Ralf Souquet.

In 1999 a dispute took place that could have threatened the future of the tournament. Until that year, the event was organized by the World Pool-Billiards Association, but the well known sports promotions company Matchroom Sport let it be known that they had wanted to become involved in staging the event. Founded by high-profile British businessman and entrepreneur Barry Hearn, Matchroom was heavily involved in promoting other sports such as snooker and fishing. But their bid to stage the World Nine-Ball Championship failed. Undeterred, Matchroom pressed ahead and staged an event it called the World Professional Pool Championship in Cardiff, Wales, in 1999. It was a televised event and was won by Efren Reyes (pictured below right). The WPS staged their own event in Alicante, Spain, which was won by Nick Varner.

As it turned out, the WPA was so impressed with the professional nature of the Matchroom event that it agreed that from that year onward it would be the official World Pool Championship. The WPA also agreed to recognize the results of the 1999 event in Cardiff. The first World Pool Championship was staged in 2000.

The Welsh capital would host the world's finest players for five successive years,

before the event moved to Taiwan in 2004 and 2005. The tournaments in 2006 and 2007 were staged in the Philippines, with Britain's Daryl Peach crowned champion in 2007.

World 9-ball billiards champion Efren 'Bata' Reyes of the Philippines lines his shot up during the Pool 15-ball individual event at the 20th Southeast Asian Games in Bandar Seri Begawan 9 August 1999.

The US Open Nine-Ball Championships

The US Open Nine-Ball Championships is one of the most prestigious tournaments in the game of pool. Held since 1976, the roll of honor reads like a who's who of the game.

The tournament has come a long way since its humble beginnings in 1976. The first event was held at Q-Masters pool room in Norfolk, Virginia, while in recent years it has been staged at the slightly grander Chesapeake Conference Center in the same state.

The tournament format is essentially based around double-elimination, with a player knocked out after losing two matches. The matches are played in races to 11, with the final being a race to 13.

Mike Sigel won the first US Open in 1976, and went on to win the event twice more. Steve Mizerak and Allen Hopkins were also among the early winners of the tournament. Earl Strickland has become a huge favorite at the US Open over the years. He still holds the record for most number of wins, with his first victory coming in 1984 and a fifth triumph sealed 16 years later in 2000.

American players have unsurprisingly dominated the event over the years, but there have been notable overseas winners. Puerto Rica's Mike Lebrón claimed victory in

1988, and the great Filipino Efren Reyes won in 1994.

In the past decade, three non-American stars have written their name in the US Open history books.

Germany's Ralf Souquet won the event in 2002, Filipino-Canadian Alex Pagulayan triumphed in 2005, and Finland's Mika Immonen was a winner in 2008 and 2009.

One of the reasons why the event is held in such high esteem by many players is its genuine "open" nature, with professionals from around the world eligible to compete. Over 250 take part in the event, simply by paying an entry fee. When you consider that from all those entrants only one man is standing at the end, you can appreciate how much satisfaction the winner gains.

Eight-Ball Tournaments

The game of eight-ball has had its own official WPA-sanctioned World Championship, which has been held in the United Arab Emirates since 2004. Efren Reyes and Ralf Souquet have both proved their all-round brilliance in the sport by winning this event.

The World Eight-Ball Pool Federation's World Championship has been staged since 1993. The tournament takes place in Blackpool, England, and has featured many of the top European stars.

The first event was won by Kevin Wright, who beat Nigel Davies in the final. Jason Twist, who lost the 1995 final to Daz Ward, won two successive titles in 2000 and

Jordan Church

Level Head

The best overall approach you can take is to try and not make too big a deal of anything that happens during a game. You should try to maintain a level head throughout.

The World Eight-Ball Pool Federation's World Championship has regularly attracted big crowds to the Imperial Hotel, in England's Blackpool, and has enjoyed big-name sponsorship in the form of Australian drinks giant Fosters. Pool fans can watch the closing stages of the event on Sky televison, and there is plenty of prestige attached to winning the main prize, especially in Britain.

2002. There were also two wins for Chris Melling, in 2001 and 2003. The event has been notable for the success of players who have also reached the highest levels of snooker. Quentin Hann was a winner in 1999, and Mark Selby triumphed in 2006.

In recent times, Gareth Potts has dominated the event. He claimed victory in 2005 as a 21-year-old, and went on to take the title twice more in 2007 and 2008. Phil Harrison won his first title with victory over Mick Hill in the 2009 final.

The last European and UK Pool Federation Eight-Ball World Championships were held in 2005, after which time the EUKPF was renamed the European Blackball Association and amalgamated under the WPA. The WPA has staged a World Blackball Championship in recent years, which was won in 2006 by Andy Lucas, and then by Wetsi Morake when it was staged two years later.

Eight-Ball Tournaments

Other Tournaments

There are a host of other major tournaments staged throughout the year, aimed at all levels of the game and taking in all its different forms. There are events in six-ball, seven-ball, and ten-ball that take place across the United States.

Alongside the major men's events, the WPA also stage a Women's World Nine-Ball Championship and a Women's US Open Nine-Ball Championship, as well as a number of other key women's tournaments throughout the year.

The International Tour has proved to be a great success, featuring a number of big eight-ball tournaments. In

recent times some of the events have been run along pro-am lines, giving decent amateur players the chance to rub shoulders with the top professionals. Fans can watch the action streamed via the internet, and relish the brilliant standard of play on show.

Across Asia, tournaments regularly take place that attract huge interest. Since 2003 the WPA has staged the Asian Nine-Ball Tour, which in 2008 alone went to China, Malaysia, Singapore, and Indonesia. The pool authorities have long since realized that they simply must keep spreading the world.

As well as regular events in six-, seven-, and ten-ball pool there are more tournaments now taking place in the games of one-pocket and bank pool, as they increase in popularity.

In many Commonwealth countries, national championships take place annually, alongside an array of other major events. In Britain, tournaments are staged at national and county level every year that attract thousands of entrants.

And then of course there are the competitions in your local bar or pub, where there may be nothing more at stake than a couple of drinks and bragging rights for a few hours. If you are playing the game of pool on a regular basis, and you are showing genuine signs of improvement, there will probably come a time when you want to take part in more than just friendly games.

Most people want that element of competition, no matter what sport they are playing. The joy truly is in taking part, but that doesn't mean you shouldn't test yourself against other good players. Good, honest competition is at the heart of the game.

Tournaments give amateur players the opportunity to rub shoulders with the world's top professionals. Fans can catch up with footage of past tournaments on the internet. Websites such as YouTube are also useful for watching trick shots in action. You may find that if you reach a decent standard you can stay on the table for many an hour in your local bar following the time-honored "winner stays on" rule.

Chapter Seven: THE RULES

The rules of pool have often provided a headache for competitors, because they can differ so significantly depending on where you play. It will never do you any harm to brush up on the officially recognized rules—here we outline the basics.

Good sportsmanship
goes hand in hand
with abiding by
the rules.

General Rules

The games of pool and billiards are played on a flat table covered with cloth and bounded by rubber cushions. The player uses a pool cue to strike a cue ball which in turn strikes object balls. The goal is to drive object balls into six pockets located at the cushion boundaries. The games vary according to which balls are legal targets and the requirements to win a match.

PLAYER'S RESPONSIBILITY

It is the player's responsibility to be aware of all rules, regulations, and schedules applying to competition. While tournament officials will make every reasonable effort to have such information readily available to all players as appropriate, the ultimate responsibility rests with the player.

LAGGING TO DETERMINE ORDER OF PLAY

The lag is the first shot of the match and determines order of play. The player who wins the lag chooses who will shoot first. The referee will place a ball on each side of the table behind the head string and near the head string. The players shoot at about the same time to make each ball contact the foot cushion, aiming to return the ball closer to the head cushion than the opponent's.

A lag shot is bad and cannot win if the shooter's ball:
(a) crosses the long string;
(b) contacts the foot cushion other than once;

(c) is pocketed or driven off the table;

(d) touches the side cushion; or

(e) the ball rests within the corner pocket and past the nose of the head cushion.

In addition, a lag will be bad if any non-object-ball foul occurs other than when balls are still moving.

The players will lag again if:

(a) a player's ball is struck after the other ball has touched the foot cushion;

(b) the referee cannot determine which ball has stopped closer to the head cushion; or

(c) both lags are bad.

PLAYER'S USE OF EQUIPMENT

The equipment must meet existing WPA equipment specifications.

In general, players are not permitted to introduce novel equipment into the game. The following uses, among others, are considered normal. If the player is uncertain about a particular use of equipment, he should discuss it with the tournament management prior to the start of play. The equipment must be used only for the purpose or in the manner that the equipment was intended.

(a) Cue Stick—The player is permitted to switch between cue sticks during the match, such as break, jump, and normal cues. He may use either a built-in extender or an add-on extender to increase the length of the stick.

(b) Chalk—The player may apply chalk to his tip to prevent miscues, and may use his own chalk, provided its color is compatible with the cloth.

Always be honest about your shots, fouls, or any other disputable plays.

(c) Mechanical Bridges—The player may use up to two mechanical bridges to support the cue stick during the shot. The configuration of the bridges is up to the player. He may use his own bridge if it is similar to standard bridges.

(d) Gloves—The player may use gloves to improve the grip and/or bridge hand function.

(e) Powder—A player is allowed to use powder in a reasonable amount as determined by the referee.

SPOTTING BALLS

Balls are spotted (returned to play on the table) by placing them on the long string (long axis of the table) as close as possible to the foot spot and between the foot spot and the foot rail, without moving any interfering ball. If the spotted ball cannot be placed on the foot spot, it should be placed in contact (if possible) with the corresponding interfering ball. However, when the cue ball is next to the spotted ball, the spotted ball should not be placed in contact with the cue ball; a small separation must be maintained. If all of the long string below the foot spot is blocked by other balls, the ball is spotted above the foot spot, and as close as possible to the foot spot.

CUE BALL IN HAND

When the cue ball is in hand, the shooter may place the cue ball anywhere on the playing surface and may continue to move the cue ball until he executes a shot. Players may use any part of the cue stick to move the cue ball, including the tip, but not with a forward stroke motion. In some games and for most break shots, placement of the cue ball may be restricted to the area behind the head string depending on the rules of the game, and then bad cue ball placement and bad play from behind the head string may apply. When the shooter has the cue ball in hand behind the head string and all the legal object balls are behind the head string, he may request the legal object ball nearest the head string to be spotted. If two or more balls are equal distance from the head string, the shooter may designate which of the equidistant balls is to be spotted. An object ball that rests exactly on the head string is playable.

STANDARD CALL SHOT

In games in which the shooter is required to call shots, the intended ball and pocket must be indicated for each shot if they are not obvious. Details of the shot, such as cushions struck or other balls contacted or pocketed are irrelevant. Only one ball may be called on each shot. For a called shot to count, the referee must be satisfied that the intended shot was made, so if there is any chance of confusion, e.g. with bank, combination and similar shots, the shooter should indicate the ball and pocket. If the referee or opponent is unsure of the shot to be played, he may ask for a call. In call shot games, the shooter may choose to call "safety" instead of a ball and pocket, and then play passes to the opponent at the end of the shot. Whether balls are being spotted after safeties depends on the rules of the particular game.

BALLS SETTLING

A ball may settle slightly after it appears to have stopped, possibly due to slight imperfections in the ball or the table. Unless this causes a ball to fall into a pocket, it is considered a normal hazard of play, and the ball will not be moved back. If a ball falls into a pocket as the result of

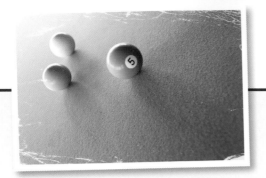

Be considerate of your opponent. Do not try to distract them while they are trying to take a shot.

such settling, it is restored as closely as possible to its original position. If a settling ball falls into a pocket during or just prior to a shot, and this has an effect on the shot, the referee will restore the position and the shot will be replayed. The shooter is not penalized for shooting while a ball is settling.

RESTORING A POSITION

When it is necessary for balls to be restored or cleaned, the referee will restore disturbed balls to their original positions to the best of his ability. The players must accept the referee's judgment as to placement.

OUTSIDE INTERFERENCE

When outside interference occurs during a shot that has an effect on the outcome

of that shot, the referee will restore the balls to the positions they had before the shot, and the shot will be replayed. If the interference had no effect on the shot, the referee will restore the disturbed balls and play will continue. If the balls cannot be restored to their original positions, the situation is handled like a stalemate.

PROMPTING CALLS AND PROTESTING RULINGS

If a player feels that the referee has made an error in judgment, he may ask the referee to reconsider his call or lack of call, but the referee's decision on judgment calls is final. However, if the player feels that the referee is not applying the rules correctly, he may ask for ruling by the designated appeals authority. The referee will suspend play while this appeal is in process. Fouls must be called promptly.

CONCESSION

If a player concedes, he loses the match. For example, if a player unscrews his jointed cue while the opponent is at the table and during the opponent's decisive rack of a match, it will be considered a concession of the match.

STALEMATE

If the referee observes that no progress is being made toward a conclusion, he will announce his decision, and each player will have three more turns at the table. Then, if the referee determines that there is still no progress, he will declare a stalemate. If both players agree, they may accept the stalemate without taking their three additional turns. The procedure for a stalemate is specified under the rules for each game.

NINE-BALL POOL

Nine-ball is played with nine object balls numbered one through nine, and the cue ball. The balls are played in ascending numerical order. The player legally pocketing the 9-ball wins the rack.

DETERMINING THE BREAK

The player who wins the lag chooses who will break the first rack. The standard format is to alternate the break.

NINE-BALL RACK

The object balls are racked as tightly as possible in a diamond shape, with the one ball at the apex of the diamond and on the foot spot and the 9-ball in the middle of the diamond. The other balls will be placed in the diamond without purposeful or intentional pattern.

LEGAL BREAK SHOT

The following rules apply to the break shot:
(a) the cue ball begins in hand behind the head string; and

(b) if no ball is pocketed, at least four object balls must be driven to one or more rails, or the shot is a foul.

SECOND SHOT OF THE RACK—PUSH OUT

If no foul is committed on the break shot, the shooter may choose to play a "push out" as his shot. He must make his intention known to the referee, and then the rules 'Wrong ball first' and 'No rail after contact' are suspended for the shot. If no foul is committed on a push out, the other player chooses who will shoot next.

CONTINUING PLAY

If the shooter legally pockets any ball on a shot (except a push out), he continues at the table for the next shot. If he legally pockets the 9-ball on any shot (except a push out), he wins the rack. If the shooter fails to pocket a ball or fouls, play passes to the other player, and if

no foul was committed, the incoming player must play the cue ball from the position left by the other player.

SPOTTING BALLS

If the 9-ball is pocketed on a foul or push out, or driven off the table, it is spotted. No other object ball is ever spotted.

STANDARD FOULS

If the shooter commits a standard foul, play passes to his opponent. The cue ball is in hand, and the incoming player may place it anywhere on the playing surface.

The following are standard fouls at nine-ball:

- *Cue ball scratch or off the table*
- *Hitting the wrong ball first*
- *No rail after contact*
- *No foot on floor*
- *Ball driven off table*
- *Touched ball*

- *Double hit/frozen balls*
- *Push shot*
- *Balls still moving*
- *Bad cue-ball placement*
- *Cue on the table*
- *Playing out of turn*
- *Slow play*

SERIOUS FOULS

For three consecutive fouls, the penalty is loss of the current rack. For unsportsmanlike conduct, the referee will choose a penalty appropriate given the nature of the offense.

STALEMATE

If a stalemate occurs, the original breaker of the rack will break again.

EIGHT-BALL

Eight-ball is played with fifteen numbered object balls and the cue ball. The shooter's group of seven balls (one through seven or nine through fifteen) must all be off the table before he

attempts to pocket the 8-ball to win. Shots are called.

DETERMINING FIRST BREAK

The player winning the lag has the option to determine who has to execute the first break shot. The standard format is alternate break.

EIGHT-BALL RACK

The fifteen object balls are racked as tightly as possible in a triangle, with the apex ball on the foot spot and the 8-ball as the first ball directly below the apex ball. One from each group of seven will be on the two lower corners of the triangle. The other balls are placed in the triangle without purposeful or intentional pattern.

If any rules are questionable, bring them up before the game has begun.

BREAK SHOT

The following rules apply to the break shot:

(a) The cue ball begins in hand behind the head string.

(b) No ball is called, and the cue ball is not required to hit any particular object ball first.

(c) If the breaker pockets a ball and does not foul, he continues at the table and the table remains open.

(d) If no object ball is pocketed, at least four object balls must be driven to one or more rails, or the shot results in an illegal break, and the incoming player has the option of

(1) accepting the table in position, or

(2) re-racking and breaking, or

(3) re-racking and allowing the offending player to break again.

(e) Pocketing the 8-ball on a legal break shot is not a foul. If the 8-ball is pocketed, the breaker has the option of

(1) re-spotting the 8-ball and accepting the balls in position, or

(2) re-breaking.

(f) If the breaker pockets the 8-ball and scratches, the opponent has the option of

(1) re-spotting the 8-ball and shooting with cue ball in hand behind the head string; or

(2) re-breaking.

(g) If any object ball is driven off the table on a break shot, it is a foul; such balls remain out of play (except the 8-ball); and the incoming player has the option of

(1) accepting the table in position, or

(2) taking cue ball in hand behind the head string.

(h) If the breaker fouls in any manner not listed above, the following player has the option of

(1) accepting the balls in position, or

(2) taking cue ball in hand behind the head string.

OPEN TABLE/ CHOOSING GROUPS

Before groups are determined, the table is said to be "open," and before each shot, the shooter must call his intended ball. If the shooter legally pockets his called ball, the corresponding group becomes his, and his opponent is assigned the other group. If he fails to legally pocket his called ball, the table remains open and play passes to the other player. When the table is "open," any object ball may be struck first except the 8-ball.

CONTINUING PLAY

The shooter remains at the table as long as he continues to legally pocket called balls, or he wins the rack by pocketing the 8-ball.

SHOTS REQUIRED TO BE CALLED

On each shot except the break, shots must be called. The 8-ball may be called only after the shot on which the shooter's group has been cleared from the table. The shooter may call "safety," in which case play passes to the opponent at the end of the shot and any object ball pocketed on the safety remains pocketed.

SPOTTING BALLS

If the 8-ball is pocketed or driven off the table on the break, it will be spotted or the balls will be re-racked. No other object ball is ever spotted.

LOSING THE RACK

The shooter loses if he

(a) *fouls when pocketing the 8-ball;*

(b) *pockets the 8-ball before his group is cleared;*

(c) *pockets the 8-ball in an uncalled pocket; or*

(d) *drives the 8-ball off the table.*

These do not apply to the break shot.

STANDARD FOULS

If the shooter commits a foul, play passes to his opponent. The cue ball is in hand, and the incoming player may place it anywhere on the playing surface.

The following are standard fouls at eight-ball:

- *Cue ball scratch or off the table*
- *Wrong ball first*
- *No rail after contact*
- *No foot on floor*
- *Ball driven off the table*
- *Touched ball*
- *Double hit/frozen balls*
- *Push shot*
- *Balls still moving*
- *Bad cue ball placement*
- *Bad play from behind the head string*
- *Cue on the table*
- *Playing out of turn*
- *Slow play*

SERIOUS FOULS

The fouls listed under Losing the Rack (see page 217) are penalized by the loss of the current rack. For unsportsmanlike conduct, the referee will choose a penalty appropriate given the nature of the offense.

STALEMATE

If a stalemate occurs, the original breaker of the rack will break again.

Differences

All pool players quickly become aware of the various differences between rules. Across America, most eight-ball players tend to play "ball in hand," where they can move the cue ball anywhere after a foul. In some parts of Europe, including Britain, eight-ball players often play with rules that state that the cue ball can only be moved if they are "foul snookered," that is to say they are unable to see both sides of any of their balls after an opponent has fouled. They can place the cue ball behind the head string in that situation. Many eight-ball players will use the rule that allows deliberate fouls to their advantage, maybe clearing an opponent's ball away from the pocket if they have various balls of their own surrounding the pocket. If you are ever told you are only allowed one shot on the black while playing blackball, challenge this—you are allowed two shots.

Always make sure you have established exactly which rules you are playing to at the start of the game.

General Rules

Index

Credits

All other images are the copyright of Quintet Publishing Limited. While every effort has been made to credit contributors, Quintet Publishing would like to apologize should there have been any omissions or errors—and would be pleased to make the appropriate correction for future editions of the book.

Quintet and the author would like to express special thanks to Jordan Church for helping with trick shots and providing tips in an exclusive interview and David Alciatore for his general expertise and invaluable guidance.

The rules on pages 208–218 are reproduced by kind permission of The Billiard Congress of America.